LifeSpeak 101: Speak Life and Win!

Wilma Hollis

All scriptures are from the New King James Version Bible unless otherwise noted.

Scripture quotations taken from the Amplified® Bible (AMPC), Copyright © 1954, 1958, 1962, 1964, 1965, 1987 by The Lockman Foundation. Used by permission. www.lockman.org

Scripture quotations taken from the Common English Bible® (CEB®), Copyright © 2011 by Common English Bible. All rights reserved.

Scripture quotations taken from the Holy Bible, 21st Century King James Version® (KJ21®), Copyright ©1994 by Deuel Enterprises, Inc., Gary, SD 57237. All rights reserved.

Scripture quotations taken from the Holy Bible, New International Version® (NIV®), Copyright ©1973, 1978, 1984, 2011 by Biblica, Inc.® Used by permission. All rights reserved worldwide.

Scripture quotations taken from The Living Bible (TLB), Copyright © 1971 by Tyndale House Foundation. Used by permission of Tyndale House Publishers Inc., Carol Stream, Illinois 60188. All rights reserved.

Scripture quotations taken from The Message (MSG), copyright © 1993, 2002, 2018 by Eugene H. Peterson. Used by permission of NavPress. All rights reserved. Represented by Tyndale House Publishers, Inc.

Cover Concept by Wilma Hollis
Cover & Interior Book Design by Cherese Agee, Rese Agee Media

The stories depicted in *LifeSpeak 101: Speak Life and Win!* are true. Names have been changed in some instances to honor the privacy of those involved.

Printed in the United States of America

ISBN: 978-0-578-88098-3 (pbk)
ISBN: 978-0-578-93277-4 (eBook)

*This book is dedicated to my personal "great cloud of witnesses":
Faye Hillman, James Hollis, Dr. Arthur M. Brazier, Alice and Homer
Hollis, Karen Haywood and Lena Akindipe. Your presence made everything
in my life so much better. And to Connor: Thank you so much for listening.*

Contents

LifeSpeak (verb)

\līf - spēk\

1. To take a promise from the Word of God that you've made your own (by meditating on it to the degree that you believe the truth that lies therein more than you believe any contradictory facts that can be comprehended by your five senses), and then to declare, speak, or decree that truth (and only that truth) regarding your circumstances with the unwavering conviction that the truth of your Word-of-God-based declaration will make the unwanted facts of your situation bow and conform to the image of your declaration. That is the truth that you are speaking.

Now, let me teach you how to lifespeak.

LifeSpeak 101: Introduction

Most Christians are not winning in life. They love God, go to church, and know lots of Bible verses, but they are not winning. The vast majority of Christians are getting defeated by the same sicknesses, broken relationships, and financial challenges as everyone else. As a result, we are left to wonder, "Where is that abundant living that Jesus said He came to give us, in John 10:10?"

Listen, we all know that life can be a difficult journey, and everyone faces tough circumstances sometimes, but why does it seem that Christians are having as difficult a time going through life's challenges as everyone else? Isn't God supposed to be on our side? If winning is supposed to be *the norm*, why does it seem, instead, to be *the exception* for so many Christians? I mean, think about it: If we were winning in overwhelming numbers, everyone would want to be a Christian, right?

According to God's Word—the Bible—you and I are supposed to win. It says you and I are destined for victory. It tells us in many verses that our battles are already won, right? Yet, frustration and discouragement come when the promises of God's Word don't match the realities of our lives. We say we believe God's Word. We want the life God has for us. But, somehow, our lives keep falling short of what the Bible says.

Aren't we supposed to be "more than conquerors" in all things? It says that in Romans 8:37. Isn't it true that "the Greater One" lives in us? It tells us this in I John 4:4. If our weeping endures for a night, where's that "joy" that was supposed to "come in the morning"? It's been promised to us in Psalm 30:5.

Sadly, many of us have been waiting for a "morning" that has never come. And, as our lives continue to fall short of what we believe and what the Bible tells us, we get more and more discouraged and frustrated.

Are you nodding your head in agreement? Can you relate to the feelings of frustration and discouragement of things not working as they "should"? Here's the real question:

Are you ready to win?

If you are tired of the areas of your life that do not reflect the victory that you know God's Word has promised you, all of that can change starting today!

Consider your purchase of this book as the equivalent of your enrollment into a "how-to" class where I'll teach you the exact steps you need to take to start turning your life around. It's time for you to stop feeling defeated. It's time for you to stop falling short of what God's Word has promised for your life. It's time for others to see all the victory you're experiencing and decide they want their lives to look like yours! Let's get started. Class is now in session. My name is Wilma Hollis, and it's my distinct honor to welcome you to:

LifeSpeak 101: Speak Life and Win!

CHAPTER ONE

The Speaker's Story

It was about 7 pm when the phone rang. I recognized the ID. It was Cassie, one of my daughters. "Hey, girl!" I answered enthusiastically, to which she responded with a sad and defeated-sounding, "Hey." "Well," I answered back, "you called, so clearly you want to talk about it, right?" (Yes, this is how I speak to my family and friends—very directly.) Then, sparks began to fly as her emotions were unleashed.

My daughter had started a new job. Her responsibilities included having to give lots of presentations. She loved preparing for the presentations. Doing the research, gathering data, building graphs and charts to illustrate complex concepts—those are her natural gifts. But it was standing in front of an audience, with all eyes staring back at her. Public speaking was not something she'd been able to master. As a matter of fact, she informed me that she'd given a presentation that very afternoon and felt she had completely (in her words) "bombed it."

"Mom," she said with a groan, "it was so awkward. I was watching my manager watching me drown in my sad attempt to present this material. And the worse part," she continued, "was that my information was on-point. My data was spot on, and everyone said so. I just flubbed the delivery of it all." Then, she waited for my response.

"Well, if you want to keep this job, and you do," I told her, "you're going to have to get better—way better—at giving presentations, right?"

She agreed. I was in teaching mode now, so I continued. "And if you're ever going to get better at giving presentations, you've got to first start by watching your words. You're going to have to stop saying that you hate public speaking. Stop saying you hate giving presentations. That's pretty basic stuff."

She was quietly receptive as I continued to assess her situation. "Now, even if you watch your words and stop saying negative things about your speaking ability, that's just the beginning. Instead of saying negative things, start saying only positive things about your speaking ability. Next, you have to do something with those negative thoughts you keep having about your ability as a public speaker. You have to use the Word of God—you'll have to meditate on it, believe it, speak it—to uproot all those I-am-an-awful-public-speaker seeds that have been planted in your mind."

(Quick note here about "other people" in your life: When you are trying to uproot negativity from your life, you cannot allow negative people in your space. While you are changing how you've been speaking about your own situation, you'll also need to stay away from others—friends, relatives, even authority figures, etc.—who tend to speak negatively about your situation.)

My daughter agreed with what I said: "Okay, I'm willing . . . no, I have to do everything you just said, but how? I mean, how do I start doing all that stuff?" She continued to share with me that there were two co-workers on her team who constantly tried to challenge her data in an attempt to embarrass her and make her seem less-than-competent. Still baffled by the outcome of the presentation, she said, "I even prayed before the presentation, and I still bombed it! So, what is it that I don't know? How do I get a handle on this? I already know that God gave me the victory over this, but I don't know. Where do I go to pick it up?" She chuckled. "Seriously, I mean, how do I get it?"

And that, my friend, is how this book came to be.

As Christians, we know, mentally, that the Bible says, "Thanks be to God who gives us the victory through our Lord Jesus Christ" (I Corinthians 15:57). We know that it says things like "you meant evil against me; but God meant it for good" (Genesis 50:20). We know the Bible says that "all things work together for good to those who love God…" (Romans 8:28). And don't forget that "…all things are possible to him who believes" (Mark 9:23). Shall I continue? I could go on and on and on with this line of thought. You probably can, too. Most of us have these verses in our heads, but do we have them deeply rooted in our hearts? If we already know all these scriptures, then why aren't they working for us? Why don't we have the victory—in our real, everyday lives—that these verses and our pastors keep telling us we already have? Why don't we see it? Why is it that we are not experiencing all this victory in practical, tangible, and visible ways?

Let's go back to my daughter's story. Cassie was feeling discouraged and defeated in three ways:

1. She had "bombed" the presentation she gave at work.
2. She prayed but failed to receive the results she'd prayed for.
3. She had haters—most of us do, even if we don't know who they are.

Remember when Cassie mentioned the two co-workers who clearly wanted her to fail? If Jesus had haters, this is something we can expect in life, too.

So, what did we do?

These were my instructions to Cassie regarding her public-speaking predicament.

1. Watch your words.

Don't agree with what you don't desire. Speak positive words only. Don't speak negative words.

I told Cassie, "Don't say another negative word about your public-speaking ability. If you can't say anything positive, keep your mouth shut." This is my advice regarding your situation, too.

Now, some of you might say, "But if your daughter was bad at public speaking, she was just bad at it. That's just the truth." And if you said that, you'd be well-intentioned but completely misinformed. Let me explain: Did Cassie "bomb" the presentation? Yes. Yes, she did. So, isn't it true that she is a terrible public speaker? No! Absolutely not! Now, is it a fact that she was not the caliber of public speaker that she wanted to be? Yes, that was a fact, but it's not the truth. Okay, hold on, now. Pay close attention here because this is where we can start changing our lives.

What we see with our physical eyes and what we experience and comprehend through our other physical senses—those are all facts. So, yes, it's a fact that Cassie didn't present well. However, the Word of God supersedes all facts. I repeat: The Word of God supersedes all facts. Here's why: God's Word is truth. God's Word is powerful, living, and unalterable; the wisdom therein is so undeniable that, with proper application, it can make any fact conform to its truth.

So, what did Cassie need to do? She needed to exchange the facts for the truth. And that's what you'll need to do, also. Use the truth to change the facts. Once Cassie understood that, she needed to go hunting. She needed to go on a treasure hunt. It was time for her to go and find the truth.

2. Find the truth.

Look for a verse of scripture (or two) that contains the truth you need to change the unwanted fact in your life.

Cassie had to search the Bible for the right verse. She needed to find the truth in God's Word that directly addressed her situation. Cassie needed to hunt for a truth that she could use to change the facts of her public-speaking outcomes. She needed to find some "I am a great public speaker" scriptures. Now, as you're reading this, you're probably thinking, "Seriously? There isn't anything in the Bible that says, 'The Lord will make you a great public speaker.'" My response to you is this: Search the scriptures. I guarantee you that God's Word was designed as a manual for living. There is no situation, no circumstance, no experience you can have in your life for which there is no scripture or Bible verse with applicable truth to get you "the win."

This is worth repeating: There is no unwanted fact, situation, circumstance, or experience in your life for which there is no applicable truth in God's Word that can get you "the win." So now, we're looking for the right scriptures. We're looking for the truth about Cassie's public speaking.

We looked at dozens of scriptures that talked about "words," "speaking," and "wisdom." See, it's a literal treasure hunt. You are looking for that verse of scripture that resonates with you. You're looking for the verse that makes your spirit leap. It contains the truth that speaks to you. You'll know it when you hear it, see it, or read it. Someone might say it to you. It could pop up in your social media feed. Your pastor may even teach on it this Sunday. It's *the* scripture you need at the moment, and you'll know it because it will be the one that addresses your problem, your concern, your challenge, your unwanted fact in a way that makes your spirit stand, take notice, and say, "Yes! That's it! That's the truth I need!" Here's the scripture that resonated with Cassie:

I'll give you the words and wisdom that will reduce all your accusers to stammers and stutters.

Luke 21:15 from The Message Bible is the scripture that addressed Cassie's fact. It was the one that would meet her need. Now, once you find the scripture, check the versions of the scripture in other translations to find the specific translation of that verse that packs the right power for you. In other words, choose the translation that best reinforces that truth for you. In this case, Cassie chose The Message Bible Version of Luke 21:15.

So, now that Cassie found the truth and the right translation of the scripture for her situation, it was time for her to take ownership of that truth. Taking ownership means taking possession of it.

You take ownership of it and make it yours so that its power will directly impact your situation. You have to take the truth and make it your truth. Remember, once you find the truth, you have to make it yours!

3. Make it yours.

Truth, in general, has power, but it has more power when it belongs and applies to you.

So, how do you take the truth and make it yours? Meditation. You elevate the truth of scripture from being the truth to being your truth through meditation.

Now, wait. Don't get spooked by the word "meditation." Meditation is simply rehearsing something by saying it over and over and over to yourself. Maybe that includes, as it often does for me, writing it over and over again. It's thinking about it, hearing it, and listening to it over and over. You get it, right?

Meditation in and of itself is neither a positive nor a negative thing. Meditation is what you make it. It's what you meditate on that makes the difference. If you meditate on evil, that's a bad thing to do. But, if you meditate on kindness, that's a good thing to do. So, the power lies in what you meditate on. Here, our focus is meditating on the truth of the Word of God. Let me share with you one of my favorite truths about the power of meditation. It's found in Joshua 1:8, and I've listed it here in three different translations of the Bible.

This Book of the Law shall not depart out of thy mouth, but thou shalt meditate therein day and night, that thou mayest observe to do according to all that is written therein. For then thou shalt make thy way prosperous, and then thou shalt have good success.
(KJ21 – 21st Century King James Version)

This Book of the Law shall not depart out of your mouth, but you shall meditate on it day and night, that you may observe and do according to all that is written in it. For then you shall make your way prosperous, and then you shall deal wisely and have good success. (AMPC – Amplified Bible, Classic Edition)

Never stop speaking about this Instruction scroll. Recite it day and night so you can carefully obey everything written in it. Then you will accomplish your objectives and you will succeed. (CEB – Common English Bible)

In each of these translations, it shows there is a direct correlation between meditating on the Word and having success or accomplishing your objectives. Meditation is the key component of this process.

Please note: Meditation is not the same as memorization. Memorization is mechanical. The goal of meditation is not to memorize, although memorization is usually a by-product of meditating on scripture. When you meditate on scripture, you're saying it to yourself. Notice, I said that you *say* it to yourself, not just *think* it to yourself. Saying it is key because faith comes by hearing the Word of God over and over, according to Romans 10:17. So, when you say it, you hear it, and when you hear it, faith comes. Faith comes for what? Faith to know that the truth of what that verse contains belongs to you. See, meditation is how you take the scripture from the page of your Bible (or the screen of your device) and get it deposited into your heart. It's how you get your subconscious to absorb the truth of God's Word. Meditation is how you make that word, verse, scripture—that truth—come alive and active for you, your life, and your circumstances. See, this is how you'll own the truth and make it yours. Meditation is how you take the seed of that verse, plant it in the soil of your heart, and continue to believe as it grows a harvest of the results you desire for your life. It all starts with meditation.

I'll explain how it works with this example:

Let's say that you've been given an electric toothbrush. You don't realize it's electric, so you brush your teeth with it as you normally would, never turning it on because you don't know there is anything to "turn on." You like the toothbrush. It's nice, but, honestly, you've wished to find a toothbrush that would give you a more complete, more thorough cleaning. You haven't found anything like that, so you continue to use what you have.

Then one day, while you're brushing your teeth, your spouse walks into the bathroom and says, "What's the matter? Is your battery dead?" In confusion, you ask, "What do you mean?" Then your spouse explains that you're brushing your teeth with an electric toothbrush, but you're not using its power. Then he or she reaches over, presses the button on your toothbrush (that you didn't know was there), and next—Wham! Your toothbrush begins to roar, buzz, and vibrate with tangible, visible force and power that you didn't even know it possessed!

Now, that's what meditating on the Word does! Meditating gets God's Word plugged into the power of your heart. Once you have abundantly planted that verse in your heart, you have the ability to speak it—because "out of the abundance of the heart, his (a man's) mouth speaks" (Luke 6:45)—with the power necessary to produce the "good success" (Joshua 1:8) and fact-changing truth you desire. Once you've meditated on it, then God's Word coming out of your mouth regarding your situation equals faith. You are actually manufacturing faith! That's what meditation does. It allows you to manufacture faith—faith to change unwanted facts of your life to God's truth. Meditation produces the faith to move mountains.

HOW DO YOU MEDITATE?

I'm going to share with you one of the ways I approach meditating on a verse. You may choose a different approach, but this is one way that has worked for me. Feel free to tailor the process in the best way that works for you.

When I approach a scripture to meditate on for the first time, I start by writing it down. Yes, I go "old school" and write it down. I have notebooks filled with pages of scriptures I've meditated on. I write the verse down over and over and over again, maybe ten or twenty times. As I'm writing it, I'm saying it. When I write a scripture, truth, or verse down, it helps to keep me from getting distracted. It keeps me focused. This process helps me establish that word as the scripture *for me*. See, as I'm writing it, I'm thinking about certain phrases to use to say it to myself. I'm looking at certain words and thinking about how they apply to my situation. Doing this helps me to take hold of it, process it, and make it mine. While I'm saying it and writing it, I'm hearing it and owning it. This method helps me claim the truth I'm meditating on. Imagine that it's like finding land and staking claim to it. That's what meditation is like. It's about transforming the verse from being the truth to being my truth.

After I spend time writing the scripture in its entirety numerous times, I usually write it in phrases multiple times. This is how I start my meditation process. After I've gone through this initial writing process, I begin to speak it. I read it aloud. I quote the verse out loud to myself. What am I doing? I am saying the Word, so I'm hearing the Word, so that the faith for that Word to become a reality in my life starts coming. Remember, Joshua 1:8 says that the Word (this Book of the Law) "shall not depart out of your mouth." That's what I'm doing. I'm making sure that the Word keeps coming out of my mouth. No matter how things look, I'm meditating on and owning my truth (the Word). No matter what anyone says, I'm meditating and owning my truth. I'm doing this "day and night" (Joshua 1:8).

Getting the Word in your heart so that it produces faith takes time and effort. How much time? How much effort? The amount of time and effort required is a personal determination, but here's how you can know that faith has come: When you realize that the truth of that verse has become more real to you than the facts of your circumstances, you know you have faith. So, after I have taken ownership of and meditated on the truth of God's Word and made it my truth, I have the faith I need to make it work for me. Now, it's time to take all that truth—all that Word—and say something. It's time to lifespeak.

WHAT DOES IT MEAN TO *LIFESPEAK?*

Lifespeaking happens when you take the truth from God's Word that you've meditated on—one in which you have developed your faith and you then "add" the narrative of whatever negative circumstances or unwanted facts are happening in your life—to create a personalized declaration. At first, you were speaking your truth only to yourself. Once you have faith, you personalize that truth by adding your life (or what's happening in your life), and you speak it or declare it publicly. That is lifespeaking.

4. LifeSpeak and win!

Incorporate the verse that you've meditated on into a personal declaration that encompasses your situation. Apply the truth you've been speaking to your life and declare it until it changes the facts to the truth! That's how you lifespeak!

Let's look at this in light of Cassie's case.

CASSIE'S TRUTH/SCRIPTURE

I'll give you the words and wisdom that will reduce all your accusers to stammers and stutters. (Luke 21:15 The Message Bible)

She took the verse she meditated on and added her life to it. Then, she turned her scripture into a declaration that she could lifespeak in order to win:

CASSIE'S LIFESPEAK DECLARATION

God, I thank you that, every time I open my mouth, you give me the words and wisdom that my accusers cannot deny or contradict. I receive this in Jesus' name, Amen.

This is Cassie's actual lifespeak declaration. See? She wrote her declaration based on the scripture she'd been meditating on. So, now, whenever she says this, it's backed by the power of faith she gained when she spent time meditating. She's not just speaking, now. Since God and His Word are one, and the Word of God is alive, Cassie is literally speaking life to her life . . . and that's how you win!

Let's review:

1. **Watch your words.** Start speaking positively and stop speaking negatively about your situation. (Keep away from others who would speak negatively in your presence, too.)

2. **Find the truth.** Search for and find a scripture or verse that resonates with you and applies to your circumstances. Be sure to use the appropriate Bible translation of that verse.

3. **Make it yours.** Meditate on the scripture until you have faith in it—until it comes alive. Meditate on it until you have more confidence in the power of the scripture than you have in your situation.

4. **LifeSpeak and win!** Create a declaration about your situation based on the scripture. Now, when you speak the Word about your situation, your truth starts changing the unwanted facts of your life.

Now that you have your Word-of-God-based declaration, you'll speak it about your life over and over and over again. You'll lifespeak every time negative thoughts come into your mind to try to convince you that nothing has changed. You'll lifespeak to anchor your soul, guard your heart, and renew your mind. Lifespeaking is how you fight the good fight of faith because the battle is in the mind. Lifespeaking is how you sharpen your personal sword of the spirit. It's like the difference between buying a suit "off the rack" and having one tailor-made to custom fit your body. You'll need to lifespeak when friends say, "You can't." You'll need to lifespeak when someone tells you, "It's too late" or "You're too young." You'll have to lifespeak when someone asks you, "Who do you think you are?" You can answer them by saying, "I'm a lifespeaker."

When you go through this process, the time and effort that you've spent with the truth in a particular scripture—no, with *your* truth . . . I say "your" truth because you've put in the time, you've meditated on that word, you've "soaked" your mind and spirit in that word, so it's *your* truth, now—the script you've developed from it and all the words you speak from your mouth relating to it . . . they all join forces to empower you to lifespeak. This means your words are infused with authority that will make the truth change the unwanted facts of whatever you're dealing with in your life. By now, you're probably wondering, "What happened to Cassie?" Well, Cassie went through the steps:

1. She *watched her words* and started speaking only positive words. She stopped speaking negative words. She stopped agreeing with things she didn't desire. She also stayed away from the negative words of others.

2. She *found the truth* and Bible translation that worked for her.

3. She *made it hers* by meditating on the verse until faith came.

4. She *started lifespeaking to win*. She spoke life to her unwanted facts. She used her truth to make those facts bow. Every time I spoke to Cassie in the weeks that followed, she never failed to talk about how God's Word was working in her. She never failed to tell me that she was an excellent speaker just waiting for the next opportunity to prove that God's Word is true.

She couldn't necessarily explain how, but she knew (in her spirit) that what she was doing and how she was speaking about her public-speaking ability had empowered her to be a great public speaker.

As the person who remembered how she sounded during her initial phone call, it was amazing to hear the power, strength, and authority in her words. She spoke of her public-speaking ability with faith, confidence, and unshakable assurance. What a difference!

Approximately two months after her initial call to me, she called again to let me know that she'd been scheduled to give another presentation. She was aware of the fact that everyone's expectations were low based on her previous performance.

Her manager had told her a number of times that if she wasn't comfortable with presenting, he would allow her to back out of it. But

Cassie continued to reassure him that she would be fine. She was also still aware of the co-workers who wanted her to fail, but they were of no consequence to her. Why? Because now, Cassie was a lifespeaker. She knew that the Word of God was so strongly and deeply rooted in her spirit that she didn't have to worry about a thing.

On the day of the presentation, as Cassie walked to the podium, she quietly spoke her truth to herself. When she faced her audience, there was no sense of nervousness or feelings of nausea that she used to feel in similar circumstances. As she stood and looked into the crowd, all she felt was an overwhelming sense of peace.

Cassie addressed that consortium of senior VP's, managers, etc., and she commanded their respect. Her data was spot on. Her delivery of the information was clear, intentional, unrushed, and professional. Everyone was pleasantly surprised.

After the presentation, she received dozens of congratulatory emails for the awesome job she had done. Her manager sent an email, along with recognition from the company, of her contribution to the team's project. Coincidence? No way! Let's take another look at the scripture and translation Cassie used.

CASSIE'S SCRIPTURE

I'll give you the words and wisdom that will reduce all your accusers to stammers and stutters. (Luke 21:15 The Message Bible)

See, when Cassie committed to lifespeak her way to excellent public-speaking skills, the result was that everyone had to acknowledge that she had given an outstanding presentation. And her accusers, the co-workers who didn't want her to succeed? They were "reduced to stammers and stutters" because even they had to admit that her presentation went phenomenally well.

And the beauty of the Word of God is this: It has no expiration date. There is no statute of limitations on God's Word and His promises. When you take the time to make a scripture your truth—to meditate on it and to build and increase your faith in it—it keeps working, keeps producing, and keeps you winning!

Since that first glorious presentation, Cassie has spoken publicly many times and has nailed it every time. She even received a promotion a few months later. Some would say it was a miracle, but it wasn't. It was intentional. Cassie took intentional steps to lifespeak and win. What about you?

What areas of your life need a win? Where have you been falling short of the victory you know you should receive on a regular basis? Are you willing? Are you ready?

You don't have to live a life that keeps you falling short of the promises of God, only to wonder if God's Word is really true. Have you ever asked yourself, "If God's Word is true, why isn't it working like this for me?"

If that's your story, let's get started because you need to know that the same steps it took for Cassie to go from zero public speaker to hero public speaker are the same steps you can use to:

- Get a better job or promotion
- Improve your marriage
- Change your financial future
- Improve your health
- Become a better parent
- Start or grow your business
- Fulfill your destiny
- And more!

Whatever area of your life is not a reflection of the promises of God is an area that you can change! And that change begins when you make the commitment to lifespeak and win!

In the next chapters, I'll share more stories of those who faced adversities, both big and small, and were able to receive the outcome they desired because they learned how to lifespeak. But first, we'll take a closer look at the four steps of how to lifespeak. We'll look at the stories of those who, in biblical times, applied the steps and received their desired outcome. You'll see through examples from Genesis and beyond how speaking the Word of God in, to, and about seemingly impossible circumstances took ordinary people to extraordinary victory. Then, you can read the stories of people just like you and me who, when faced with the option to give in to the naysayers, experts, and negative circumstances, made the choice to lifespeak. They learned to speak life to their lives and win!

Let's go!

CHAPTER TWO

The Four Steps

I t is impossible to overemphasize the impact of the words we speak regarding our own lives. For example, have you ever been around someone who constantly said they were tired? If your answer is "yes," you can probably attest to the fact that they are usually sluggish and constantly in need of sleep, right? But, what if that same person, instead of saying "I'm tired" all the time, said something else? What if they began to say, "I'm energized, excited, and ready! I'm thrilled about what's next for me." What would happen if they said that? What would happen if you started saying it? As you are about to find out, speaking energy will bring energy just as speaking tiredness will only make you more tired.

Step One: WATCH YOUR WORDS.

We must be mindful of the words we speak. As we explore the need to watch our words, which is Step One in the LifeSpeak 101 process, we'll take a look at three categories of speaking. If you want to win in every area of your life (and you can), you are going to have to . . .

Watch what you say:

- About your circumstances to others
- To others in response to their words
- To yourself about your circumstances

Watch what you say about your circumstances to others.

The ultimate example of how to watch your words regarding your circumstances is provided by God Himself. As we are learning how to change the circumstances in our lives that are not consistent with the promises of God, the following lesson is key: Do not agree with circumstances you don't desire. We can see an example of this if we look at how God handled a situation He wanted to change. In order to do this, we have to go all the way back to the beginning. I mean the beginning of everything, as in the story of creation in the book of Genesis. In Genesis 1:1-3, it says, basically, that there was darkness. It's clear, based on what God said in verse three, that He didn't want everything to remain in darkness. But you know what isn't so clear? What isn't easily noted is what God didn't say. God didn't comment on the darkness. He never said, "Man, oh, man! Can you believe how dark it is out here? It's so dark. I can't even see my hand in front of my face!" No! God never said anything about the darkness! Why not? Because He wouldn't waste words to comment on or agree with a circumstance He wanted to change.

Instead of commenting on the darkness, you know what God did? He said, "Let there be light." And what happened? There was light. The light responded to God's words. And what did light do? Light came. And, if you continue to read the story of creation, you'll see that when God wanted to change something, He said something. He called it the way He wanted it to be, not how it was. He didn't comment on the way things were. He spoke only what he desired. He spoke words to create what He wanted. God spoke what He wanted to see, not what He saw.

Throughout the story of creation, you'll see the words "and God said" over and over again. And what was God saying? He was saying everything He wanted to see. So, just like God, you are going to have to watch your words. Make sure you are saying *to* your circumstances and *in* your circumstances only what you desire to *be* your circumstances.

Watch what you say to others in response.

Many times in life, we share our desires and dreams with those who are not equipped to handle them. We'd like to think that everyone would be happy and supportive of our desire for positive change, but that's not always the case. A perfect example of this can be found in the Bible, where a young boy named Joseph shared his dreams with his ten older brothers. He had a dream that one day, he'd be a ruler, and they would have to bow to him. When Joseph shared his dream with his brothers, they basically said, "Who do you think you are?"

When we're working to change a circumstance in our lives or aspire to become more, not everyone will cheer us on. So, you'll need to know what to say when the words of others (which may even include your family and friends) try to talk you out of the dreams, plans, and positive changes you desire to make in your life. What do you say in response to those who have negative opinions about your dreams and goals?

How will you respond when they ask you the question, "Who do you think you are?"

Let me start by encouraging you to seek God's wisdom regarding with whom you share information about your life . . . any information. Of course, I understand that there are times when others will know— maybe even need to know—your circumstances, and you'll have to know what to say or how to respond. Let's look at what happened to a ruler named Jairus when people spoke against what he desired. How did Jesus advise him? Let's take a look at the synopsis of the story that's found in the eighth chapter of Luke.

Luke 8:41-42 Jairus, a ruler from the synagogue, comes to Jesus, asking him to come to his house and heal his only daughter. She is twelve years old.

Jairus and Jesus are in the middle of a large crowd, so everyone sees and hears Jairus' request. He even bows before Jesus in humble submission, in front of everyone. This is not normal behavior for someone of such great stature. I believe Jesus was moved by his humility.

Luke 8:43-48 But as Jairus and Jesus are headed to the ruler's home, their journey gets interrupted by a woman who needed to be healed.

Luke 8:49-50 Right after the woman explains that she's been healed by touching Jesus' clothes, Jesus tells her to go in peace (we will talk more about this woman later). As He and Jairus resume their journey to the ruler's home, a messenger arrives on the scene with breaking news for Jairus: "Your daughter is dead. No need to bother Jesus, now. It's over."

Luke 8:50 Here's what I love about this verse: Before Jairus could respond to the news that his daughter has died, Jesus tells him three things. "One, do not be afraid. Two, only believe. Three, if you obey instructions one and two, your daughter will be made whole." That's good advice for all of us.

See, what the "news reporter" was really saying was, "It's too late." He was saying, "Stop believing. It's no use. Your daughter is gone. It's hopeless. You've already lost her." But Jesus had another plan.

Is there an area of your life that you've been hoping to get healed? Whether you desire a better marriage, more opportunities for your business, a healthier body, etc., I'm sure you know people who will try or have tried to talk you out of it. Maybe you've decided to apply for a promotion at work, but your co-worker says things like, "It's too late. They never promote us. I heard they've already chosen the person they want to promote, anyway. What's the use? You're not connected enough to get the promotion." Remember the words of Jesus: "Do not be afraid . . . only believe." Also, please recognize this truth: You don't have to respond to everything that is said to you. There are times when more faith is demonstrated by your silence than by trying to convince a naysayer that God is able. Just keep believing and let the outcome speak for itself. See, Jesus was telling Jairus, "Shhhh! Say nothing. Fear not. Only believe." You don't have to argue with your naysayers. You just have to stay in faith. Your winning results will be all the responses you'll need.

Luke 8:51 Look at what Jesus did in this verse. When he arrives at

Jairus' home, he only allows certain people to come inside the house with him. You have to make sure you only let certain people "in on" what you're believing for regarding your life, too.

Luke 8:52 All the people in the house are crying and weeping, but Jesus, in spite of how it looks, makes no comment that agrees with her being dead. He doesn't try to comfort the mourners. He doesn't give his condolences. No, not at all. Instead, he says, "Stop crying. She's not dead. She's asleep."

Luke 8:53-54 All the mourners stop crying and start laughing at Jesus' words. There may be times when people laugh at you, too. But so what? As they laughed, Jesus put them out of the house. Why? Because He only wanted certain people, people who believed, to be in the presence of Jairus' little daughter.

Luke 8:54 Then Jesus spoke. He said what He desired. He spoke what Jairus believed him for and asked him to do. He spoke these life-giving, life-restoring, death-defying words: "Little girl, arise."

Luke 8:55-56 Jairus' prayers were answered. It wasn't too late. His daughter wasn't dead; she was alive. All this happened because Jesus stopped Jairus from responding to the messenger's negative news. It is always better to say nothing than to speak against your desired outcome. So, what should you say and do in response to the words of others? First, fear not. Do not be afraid. Next, keep on believing. Then, keep saying what you desire. Continue to speak your desired outcome.

At this point, you know how to watch what you say *to your circumstances*, and you know how to watch what you say *in response to others and what they say about your circumstances*. Now, it's time for us to learn how to conquer our biggest challenge in this area. Our biggest challenge is to watch what we say *to ourselves*.

Self-talk can be the most damaging or most life-affirming communication we hear on a consistent basis. What are you regularly saying to yourself? What's the conversation that is taking place in your head about you right now? In order for you to change things in your life that no longer serve you, you must begin to say the right things to yourself about yourself and your circumstances. Don't allow negative thoughts to float aimlessly in your mind. Pay attention to what you're thinking. Instead of talking yourself out of the awesome plans God has for your life, you should talk yourself into those awesome plans. Remember that woman who touched Jesus' clothes? Well, let's take a closer look at her story by reading the account provided in Mark 5:25-34. We discover in this passage that it's about a woman who had a whole lot of problems.

There were so many things she wanted to change about her life; it probably seemed impossible. If you think you've got issues, take a look at her story. Here's an itemized list of her circumstances:

Mark 5:25-34

1. She was very sick from hemorrhaging for twelve years.
2. She was in financial ruin from spending all her resources on doctors.
3. The doctors were ineffective and couldn't help her.
4. Instead of getting better, her condition grew worse.
5. It was against the law for women to go in public when they were bleeding in that way. Therefore, she was an outcast.
6. She was committing a criminal act just by being in the crowd. This is similar to the way that those with leprosy were treated. She could have been put to death for exposing others.

Watch what you say to yourself.

It is clear that this woman had a lot of "issues." Yet, in spite of how badly things were going in her life, it was what she kept saying to herself that made all the difference. It was by constantly speaking to herself about the outcome she desired instead of the circumstances she was enduring that she was able to turn her entire life around. Do you see what she kept saying?

According to Mark 5:28, "For she said, "If only I may touch His clothes, I shall be well." That's what she kept saying, but who was she talking to? Remember, she was an outcast. No one was with her. She didn't have her BFF helping her get through the crowd because that would make them an accomplice. So, who was she talking to as she dragged her iron-deficient, weakened body through the crowd to get to Jesus? We find the answer where this same story is told by Matthew in the ninth chapter. In Matthew 9:21, it tells us who she was talking to. It says, "For she said within herself, If I may but touch his garment, I shall be whole."

She was talking to herself. She was speaking to herself. This was the conversation that was being carried on in her mind. This was her self-talk. These were the words she spoke inside herself that pushed her beyond the barrier of all the problems she had. It was her self-talk that helped her ignore her painful past and believe for a better future. It was the words she spoke to herself over and over and over and over again. As she pressed her way through the crowd, I believe she just kept saying it. I believe she was saying it with her mouth and thinking it in her mind. "If I can just touch his garment, I'll be made whole." Can you see her in your mind's eye? She's sick, weak, pale, and scared. There were so many reasons to give up. But, with every step, she kept saying to herself, "If I can just touch his clothes, I will be made whole."

(As I type these words on my outdated desktop, I'm speaking to myself, too. I'm saying, "Just keep writing. Your words will touch far more people than your hands ever will. Just keep writing. This book will be a blessing far beyond anything you could ever imagine. Just keep writing. Your words will help people and bring glory to God.")

This woman had every reason to just stop, go home, and die, but *no!* She believed that there was more for her life, and she gave her all in pursuit of it. Can you relate? Do you realize that's true about your life, too? You know God has more for you than what you are living today. You know it. Even if you're not willing to admit it yet, you know. That's why you must watch what you say to yourself. Yes, our words have power. But our words have the most power and impact on ourselves.

So, what happened? The woman who had been hemorrhaging for 12 years was able to touch Jesus' garment and was healed immediately. When Jesus felt healing flow from his body, he turned to her and said, "Your faith has made you whole." She received what she believed. She believed what she said to herself. Now, don't miss this. Not only was she healed, but she was also made "whole." Jesus told her to "go in peace." Peace means wholeness. It means nothing missing, nothing broken, nothing lacking. I believe that Jesus didn't just heal her body. I believe not only was her health restored, but her finances were, too. Jesus honored her words, and He made her whole.

Isn't it about time for you to be made whole, too? What are you saying to yourself about your current situation? Please, get this: If you desire to change your life and whatever negative circumstances you are facing, you must stay in control of your self-talk. You must monitor the words you speak to yourself.

Step Two: FIND THE TRUTH.

I used to have a pastor who, whenever you asked him a question, would ask you a question right back. No matter what question you asked him, his answer would start with this: "What does the Word of God say about it?"

The Bible, which is the Word of God, tells us the will of God. If you want to know the will of God, all you have to do is search the Word of God. The Bible is really a manual for living by faith. If we are to successfully live by faith as we are instructed in II Corinthians 5:7, which says, "For we walk by faith and not by sight," then we must start with the truth. So, first, let's define the truth.

But, before we go further, I must make a point: This book is written to those who already believe that the Bible is the Word of God. I am not trying to convince you that it is. I am writing this book to an audience of believers who are fully persuaded that God's Word is the truth, the final authority, the God-inspired truth recorded by men. That is the premise from which this book is written. Now that we have that settled, let's continue.

In the book of John chapter 17, Jesus knows that the time for his crucifixion is rapidly approaching. He knows that the days ahead are going to be difficult, not only for him but also for his disciples. So, Jesus lifts his eyes toward heaven and begins to pray. In John 17:17, He asks God to "sanctify them by Your truth; Your word is truth."

After you decide to watch what you say about any area you want to change in your life, next you have to find the truth about it. As Jesus prayed to God in John 17:17, He said, "Your word is truth." If you want to find the truth about any circumstance in your life, you'll find it in God's Word.

John 8:32 puts it this way: "And you shall know the truth and the truth shall make you free." When you have a situation in your life that does not agree with what God's Word says, it means that your circumstances are not the truth. They may be the facts—maybe even unwanted facts—but they are not the truth. So, to change the facts, we must find the truth. We must find the applicable truth that will change our facts by searching God's Word. Let's get started.

As an example, let's say you have a business. You've done everything you know to do, but your business is not growing. First, remember to watch what you say. Please, don't say things like, "Business is really slow" or "I'm not sure we'll make it." Okay, so you're watching your words. Good. Now, let's find some truth. You'll have to go to the Word of God and find out what God's Word says about your business. Let's start with these verses:

3 John 2 - *Beloved, I pray that you may prosper in all things, and be in health, just as your soul prospers.*

Psalm 115:14 - *May the Lord give you increase more and more, you and your children.*

Isaiah 48:17 - *I am the LORD, your God, Who teaches you to profit, Who leads you by the way you should go.*

Now, this is the truth. This is the Word of God. This is the will of God for you. The Bible has various translations, so once you have found a verse that addresses your unique circumstances, find the translation of that verse that best speaks to you. This is the truth that you'll use to change the unwanted facts about your business and your life and have them conform to the truth of God's Word. Next, you're going to take this truth and make it yours!

Step Three: MAKE IT YOURS.

If you asked me, "Do you know NBA legend, LeBron James?" I would probably say, "Yes, of course, I know who he is." But if you persisted and asked, "But do you really know him?" I'd answer, "No, I do not, personally, know LeBron James." Do you know what this also means? It means that LeBron James doesn't personally know me, either. See the difference?

This same principle applies to scripture, but many Christians don't make the connection. Just because you can quote or recite a scripture or verse, that doesn't mean that you know it or that it knows you. Many Christians believe that if they can recite a scripture, that it's supposed to work for them. The reality is that they know scriptures the way I know LeBron James. Most of us know LeBron James because he is famous. Well, scriptures can be famous or popular, too. A lot of people may know what a verse says or where it's located, but they don't really know it.

What would it take for me to be able to say I *really* know LeBron James? It would take time. We'd have to spend time together. We'd have to get to know one another. And then, after we really got to know each other and became friends, if he called on me or I called on him, we'd both know that the other would answer because that's what real friends do. No questions asked.

That same principle applies to scripture. Getting to know the truth of God's Word takes time. You may know what a verse says or where it is, but if you haven't spent time with it, it's not really yours. Do you have a right to it? Yes, of course! You may know of it, but it doesn't know you.

So how do you make *the truth* (which is an applicable scripture from God's Word that you can use to deal with your specific circumstance) *your truth*?

Psalm 119:97 says, "O, how I love Your law! It is my meditation all the day."

I Timothy 4:15 says, "Meditate on these things; give yourself entirely to them, that your progress may be evident to all."

John 15:7 says, "If you abide in me and My words abide in you, you will ask what you desire, and it shall be done for you."

Proverbs 4:20-21 says, "My son, give attention to my words; incline your ear to my sayings. Do not let them depart from your eyes; Keep them in the midst of your heart."

Psalm 119:15 says, "I will meditate on Your precepts, and contemplate Your ways."

Do you see the common element in these verses? It's meditation. While not all the verses use the word meditation, take a look at John 15:7. It uses the word "abiding" in you. How do you get the word to abide? Meditation. Look at Proverbs 4:20-21. If the word is before your eyes and in your heart, that means you've been meditating on it.

Meditation is the way you take the truth from God's Word and make that truth yours. According to Noah Webster's 1828 American Dictionary of the English Language, meditate means "to dwell on anything in thought; to contemplate; to study; to turn or revolve any subject in the mind." Meditation of God's Word increases your faith and strengthens your belief in it. More faith equals more power.

Remember: The goal of meditating on God's Word is to make it more real to you than your circumstances, problems, or unwanted situation.

Hebrews 11:1 says, "Now, faith is the substance of things hoped for, the evidence of things not seen." See, faith comes by hearing the Word of God over and over and over again. That's what Romans 10:17 means. Faith comes by hearing, not by having heard. That's why you have to keep hearing it, keep reading it, keep speaking it. Think of it as being similar to the role gas plays for your car. In order for your car to work, you have to keep gas in the tank. You can't fill your tank once and expect to never take it to the gas station for the next three months. That would be ridiculous, right?

Here's another example:

Let's say I bought you a new car and said that I left the keys on the table. I'm sure you'd be excited. Now, imagine if you forgot to retrieve the keys from the table and, instead, you ran outside and jumped in the driver's seat. You'd soon realize something's missing. You wouldn't be able to go anywhere because you forgot the keys. *The Word of God is the vehicle for your life. Meditation is the key that gets the Word of God to take you where you want to go. If you want the Word of God to take you away from an unwanted circumstance in your life, you've got to get the key! You've got to meditate on the Word!* (You should stop and re-read the last four sentences.)

When the truth of God's Word is meditated *on*, it creates faith. Meditation is how faith is built. It starts the engine of the Word of God. It energizes the Word for you, personally! It's by meditating on God's Word that you take *the truth* and make it *your truth*.

Step Four: LIFESPEAK AND WIN!

Once you've meditated on the truth to the degree that it is more real to you than your circumstances, you have faith. When you know that your confidence in the truth is stronger than the lies and unwanted facts of your circumstances, you have faith. And you know what faith does? Faith speaks. Faith spoken gives life. Faith spoken is life received. Now, you can lifespeak and win!

Every time you speak of your situation, you're lifespeaking. Lifespeaking means you are declaring the truth of God's Word about your circumstances even in the face of contradiction. No matter how negative your circumstances may appear, you're going to continue to lifespeak.

As a result, the truth of your words will make the facts of your situation bow until they align with what you are saying—or lifespeaking.

If you think this is something new, it isn't. I can provide you with countless examples from the Bible of those who, in the face of perilous circumstances, chose to lifespeak with unapologetic courage and boldness. We've looked at a few, but here are some others:

I Samuel 17:46

This day will the Lord deliver you into my hand, and I will strike you and take your head from you. And this day I will give the carcasses of the camp of the Philistines to the birds of the air and the wild beasts of the earth, that all the earth may know that there is a God in Israel.

Wow! That's lifespeaking! Imagine David, a young shepherd boy, facing Goliath, the giant, and telling him he is going to cut off his head and feed his carcass to the vultures. It's no wonder Goliath laughed at him. To Goliath, David must have looked like an ant. He even called him a dog! But what Goliath didn't realize was that David was lifespeaking. Goliath's giant-size body was no match for David's giant-size faith.

Daniel 3:1-30

What about Daniel's friends, Shadrach, Meshach, and Abednego? They were all chosen to train and serve in the king's palace. King Nebuchadnezzar issued a decree that, when all the people heard music, they were commanded to fall down and worship the golden image that King Nebuchadnezzar had set up or get thrown into a fiery furnace. But Shadrach, Meshach, and Abednego had a prior commitment. They were committed to worshiping God, and Him only. When faced with the threat of certain death, this is how they responded: "Our God whom we serve is able to deliver us... and He will deliver us from your hand, O King. But if not, let it be known to you... we do not serve your gods, nor will we worship the gold image which you have set up." What were they telling the king? We will not bow! They declared their deliverance even before they were thrown into the fiery furnace. Now, that's lifespeaking! That's making God's Word the final authority on the matter.

What about Jesus? Time and time again, He demonstrates to us the power of lifespeaking in the face of seemingly insurmountable odds.

Matthew 8:23-27

The disciples are afraid of a storm and think they are going to die.

1. Jesus is asleep (peace in the midst of the storm).

2. When they wake him up, he rebukes the winds and waves.

3. Immediate calm ensues.

John 11:38-44

Sisters Martha and Mary tell Jesus that if he had come sooner, their brother, Lazarus, would not have died. At this point, Lazarus had been dead and buried for three days. Martha tells Jesus that after all this time, the body probably stinks. Martha and Mary thought it was too late.

1. Jesus tells them, "Did I not say to you that if you would believe you would see the glory of God?"

2. Then, Jesus calls out to Lazarus, "Lazarus, come forth."

3. Lazarus comes out of the burial cave, wrapped in burial garments.

4. Jesus' next instructions are, "Loose him, and let him go."

Luke 5:1-9

Simon Peter loans Jesus the use of his boat for Jesus to teach from just beyond the shore. In gratitude, Jesus tells Simon Peter to launch his nets into the deep in preparation for a great catch. Simon Peter had fished all day and caught nothing, but he launches his net at Jesus' words.

1. Jesus knew Simon Peter had fished all day and caught nothing.

2. Still, Jesus promised him a great catch.

3. The catch was so great that Simon Peter's net broke, and he had to call friends to help him haul in the load.

In none of these instances was Jesus, or any of the other lifespeakers mentioned, intimidated by what they saw, what they heard, what they were told, or even what they felt. They spoke the desired outcome in the face of adversity. They spoke what they desired in the presence of contradiction and even ridicule. This is how you lifespeak. This is how you win!

Friend, what I've just shared with you isn't something I've heard. This is how I live.

Now, let me be clear: This is in no way meant to imply that my life is perfect. It means that in every unwanted circumstance, this is how we walk by faith and not by sight. So many Christians, when they find themselves facing adversity, love to quote the verse from Isaiah 54:17 that says, "No weapon formed against you shall prosper." It's a powerful verse, but let me point out that the weapons will, indeed, form. As long as you're on this journey called "life," you will encounter adversity. Again, weapons will form. The promise provided in Isaiah 54:17 is that the weapons that form will not prosper. They won't be successful. Why not?

The reason the weapons formed against you won't prosper is because you are going to lifespeak. You are going to speak the Word of God to the storms of your life and witness the calming of the winds and waves of your adversity.

If you are tired of praying without certainty, keep reading. If you are exhausted from hoping things will change just because you are a Christian instead of knowing that your words have power, keep reading.

I'm going to share with you the stories of those who took the exact steps we've just reviewed and elevated their lives from unwanted facts to winning ways. I'll share a few of my own stories, too, that allowed me and my family to defy medical odds, beat anxiety, and lifespeak our way to winning. Are you ready?

Let's hear the stories of those who have lived the lessons of LifeSpeak 101 and learned how to speak life to their lives . . . and WIN!

CHAPTER THREE

Deena's Story

I t was 2009. I was a member of a prayer group that met at a neighbor's house every other week. One morning, our host and group leader, Missy, informed us that she had spoken to another mom, Deena, at her son's school and told her about our group. Although she didn't know Deena very well, Missy believed she should invite Deena to join us, and so she did.

That morning, Deena showed up at our meeting looking worried, drained, exhausted, and defeated. I didn't know her at the time, but she struck me as an elegant woman who seemed as if she was on her last leg. This lady was in a battle with life, and it was obvious to all of us that she was not winning.

Missy began our meeting by telling her that, whatever was going on in her life, we were all there to help. Missy also told her that if she was okay with it, she could let us know if there was anything that she needed so that we could start praying for her. I remember thinking that this woman was dealing with something that had made her fragile. She was fragile in a way that made it seem as though the very next thing could send her over the edge. I've been there. That's why I recognized it.

Deena began to cry a little as she explained that her oldest son, Evan, had a drug addiction. She and her husband had spent tens of thousands of dollars over the years on rehabilitation centers, treatment programs, counselors, therapists, and experts, but nothing had worked.

Evan, the oldest of her three children, had lied, stolen, and misled them in various ways, over and over again, to get money for his addiction. His relationship with his siblings was nonexistent. No one in the family trusted him anymore. They had kicked him out of the house numerous times. He had lived in shelters and in cars. He'd been homeless. There were times when they had tried "tough love" and refused to give him money. That didn't work, either. On top of it all, the impact of the situation on Deena's marriage was catastrophic.

The devastation that Evan's addiction had wreaked upon her family was incalculable. Deena spoke for almost an hour, pausing to cry as she gave a verbal inventory of what this addiction was costing her family. Occasionally, she'd say, "You all seem like very nice people, but the truth is, I can't believe I'm sharing all of my family problems with a group of complete strangers."

When she finished, we told her that we were going to pray for her and with her. She smiled in a polite but disbelieving way. It was clear that she thought we were very kind but extremely naive. She and her family had been in this battle for a number of years, and they expected nothing more than for things to continue going downhill. She thanked us and agreed to let us pray, but she added, "I've been prayed for by so many people, so many times, and it has never worked. This is just something we have to deal with. It just never works, but okay."

I'll never forget the image of Deena sitting in a La-Z-Boy chair as all these women (about seven of us) surrounded her, some with a hand on her shoulder, and prayed. What did we pray? We asked God to give her strength, wisdom, courage, and endurance to stand on His Word. We asked Him to help her receive peace and restoration for her family and deliverance for her son from the horrendous addiction. We prayed for strength for her marriage and reconciliation between the siblings. We asked God to heal her family.

After we prayed, we all sat and talked for a while. The compassion we all felt for her was palpable, and while prayer was the right place to start, it was only the beginning. Next, we had to give her some specific instructions. It's important to remember that once you've prayed, the real faith fight begins right after you say, "Amen." So, we needed to talk to her about how to fight this fight of faith that we were now all in together.

We began by assuring her that our prayers for her were based on God's Word and that God's Word would never fail, so no matter what happens, what you're told, how long it takes, or even how things look— especially when it looks as if he's getting worse—watch your words. Our main piece of advice was, "Never again say that Evan has an addiction."

Now, some of you may say that those instructions are ridiculous. You may even say that it doesn't make sense. And the truth is, this doesn't make sense; it makes faith. The addiction was a fact, an unwanted fact, but it was not the truth. We are now turning our backs on the facts and fixing our eyes, our words, our hearts, our minds, our everything, on the truth. That's what you have to do in order to get the win.

Listen, Deena and her family had already tried everything they knew, and it all failed. It was time for her family to get the victory God's way. It was time for them to learn to lifespeak.

Deena's words were going to matter now more than ever! So, it was important that going forward, she had to stick to the plan and follow the steps, and the same goes for you. Remember to:

1. **Watch your words.** Deena had to speak positive words only. She had to stop saying negative words. Deena couldn't say anything that agreed with what she didn't desire. So, never again could she say, "Evan has an addiction."

2. **Find the truth.** We provided Deena with many of the truths and scriptures we had prayed (along with their translations) and encouraged her to really dive into the Word of God and His promises. She was going to have to take ownership of those promises.

3. **Make it yours.** We encouraged Deena to make those scriptures hers by meditating, contemplating, and speaking those truths (to herself) over and over. This was an on-the-job-

training, crash-course-in-faith situation for Deena. She had no time to start from ground zero. She and her family needed help, and they needed it yesterday. Her son's life was depending on this process. We explained that she was going to have to keep God's Word in her heart, on her mind, and coming out of her mouth concerning this matter. And she was going to have to do this no matter what!

For Deena, this was like building a house in the middle of a hurricane. But she wasn't alone in the fight. We were all in this fight together. (This is a great place to point out the value of having friends who can help you pray. You need friends who can pray with you. And, when you can't pray for yourself, you need friends who can pray for you. The Bible calls this "standing in the gap." See Ezekiel 22:30.)

Deena took the process seriously. When she left us that day, she was changed. The woman who she was when she had walked in a few hours earlier wasn't the same woman who walked out. Deena had entered the house defeated, desperate and discouraged. Now, she had hope.

Deena took the scriptures we gave her and meditated on them. She and her husband prayed them, read them, quoted them, declared them. Those verses were transformed from being the truth to becoming their truth. They believed the verses more than they believed the addiction that was trying to destroy their son, their marriage, and their family. See, the reason you do this is because the Word of God anchors your soul when the waves of your stormy circumstances start crashing into your mind to make you give up. There was no quitting for Deena and her husband now. They were anchored in the Word of God.

4. **LifeSpeak and win!** Deena and her husband took those scriptures they had meditated on and then tailored a declaration based on what was happening in their lives. This is what they began to lifespeak:

"Jesus is Lord over Evan's life. Evan is free and delivered from addiction because greater is He that lives in Evan than he (or anything else) that is in the world. So, we declare that Evan is free, delivered, and a man of God."

That was it. That was the outcome where Deena and her family decided to stake their claim. They were going to stand on this declaration no matter what happened until they saw Evan's life align with every word of it. Now, if you're looking for this to be an overnight, happily-ever-after, success-in-sixty-minutes story, you won't find that here. For the next two, almost three years, we all fought the good fight of faith for Evan to overcome the addiction that had haunted him for so many years. And, no matter what was happening with him, no matter what the facts were regarding the current state of his behavior, we called Evan "a man of God." When Evan was homeless, we called him "a free, delivered man of God." When Evan called Deena and cursed her out because she refused to send him money, we called him "a free, delivered man of God." When he told his parents he hated them and never wanted to see them again, we prayed and called him "a free, delivered man of God." When he threatened to take his own life, we prayed and called him "a free, delivered man of God."

It was painful for Deena and her family, but she and her husband continued to lifespeak concerning Evan. All of us continued to hang onto the truth of the Word of God, knowing that the facts would have to bow because we were standing in faith for Evan. We never stopped calling Evan "free." We were relentless in our declaration of Evan's deliverance. We were persistent, determined, and unwavering as we continued to call Evan "a man of God." We were all lifespeaking Evan back to life . . . but not back to life before the addiction. No! We were lifespeaking Evan back to the life God had planned for him. We were calling on him to fulfill his destiny. No matter how hopeless the circumstances seemed, Deena was determined. She was convinced that the truth of God's Word was stronger and more powerful than the facts of the addiction that plagued her son.

So, listen, you can't give up, either! It might take a week, two years, a decade, whatever! You have to lifespeak until you get the win. You have to lifespeak all the way to your victory! You can't just do this for a week and pat yourself on the back. No! You'll have to do this when it looks as if things are changing for the better and when it looks like things are getting worse. You lifespeak God's Word every day, all day, no matter what anyone says. That's what you have to do. That's the difference between the people who see what they've been saying (declaring) and the people who just keep saying what they see. You can make things change by standing on God's Word. Deena did it. And you can too! So, do you want to know what happened with Evan, Deena, and the rest of the family?

The facts in Evan's life had to bow to the truth of God's Word. Evan beat his addiction. And that's not all. He gave his life to Christ. And that's not all. He returned to college. And that's not all. Evan graduated with honors. Are you getting this? This is the power that's available to you when you lifespeak. Evan is now a "free, delivered man of God."

His life has purpose, and his future is bright. Deena's marriage and family were restored, too. Her children love and trust each other again. See, Evan is living proof that when you understand that the truth of God's Word is stronger than the facts, you can speak life to your life! No matter how dire the situation looks, this is a real-life example that you, too, can lifespeak and make every area of your life reflect the victory that God's Word has guaranteed. It was true for Deena and her son, Evan, and it is true for you. Believe it! You can lifespeak. You can speak life to your life and win!

CHAPTER FOUR

Kim's Story

Kim, my next-door neighbor at the time, had misplaced her cell phone. This happened when our children were still very young. Kim and I were in the backyard watching our children play as she described all the places that she had checked in her attempt to find it. When she finished reciting her long list, I chimed in with a verbal list of my own: "Sofa cushions? The comfy chair? Jacket and jean pockets? Both cars? The kid's playroom? Tara's house? Beth's house?" It turns out she was right. Kim had, indeed, looked *everywhere*.

It was around this time that I had been "practicing" how to have faith in God's Word. I was really learning how to use it, in practical ways, to transform every area of my life. While Kim was lamenting the difficulties of life without her cell phone and how she really didn't want to deal with the hassle of buying another one, it hit me! The Word of God works where you apply it, right? It works where you *apply it*, not where you *hear it*, not where you *learn it*, and not even where you *memorize it*. The Word of God works where you apply it. Faith without works (or application) is dead.

But wilt thou know, O vain man, that faith without works is dead?
—James 2:20 (KJV)

The Living Bible translates James 2:20 like this:

Fool! When will you ever learn that 'believing' is useless without doing what God wants you to? Faith that does not result in good deeds is not real faith."

So, I said to her, "Hey, Kim, I can help you get your cell phone back if you want." Being Kim, she responded, "Well, if I didn't think you'd help, I wouldn't have mentioned it to you at all. How? Do you have it?" As I was trying to stop laughing at her quick wit and suspicious expression, I answered, "Of course I don't have it. But," I continued, "before I help you, you have to make me a promise."

Now, the way Kim looked at me, I could tell she was thinking, "What are you up to, girl?" She slowly responded, "OOOOOOkay?" Then, I told her that, in order for this to work, she had to *watch her words*. Kim had to promise me that she would stop saying she couldn't find her cell phone. She had to promise me that every time she thought about her cell phone, she would thank God for showing her the truth regarding where her cell phone was located.

I had done this very thing with a set of misplaced keys a few days earlier, but I'd forgotten about it when Kim initially mentioned her missing cell phone predicament.

Well, Kim needed her cell phone, and she needed it now! So, she promised me that, going forward, she would *watch her words* and not say she couldn't find her cell phone. She also promised that whenever she was tempted to say anything like that, she would, instead, say, "Thank you, God, for leading me to the truth of where my cell phone is located." Notice here that I'm telling Kim to watch her words and stop agreeing with what she didn't desire. Stop repeating your unwanted fact. Stop speaking "my-cell-phone-is-missing" words.

Next, we needed to *find the truth*. Well, I already had the truth she needed—the scripture was one I'd been meditating on. It was the same scripture I had used to find my keys. See, sometimes God will lead you to focus on and meditate on a scripture that seems to have no relevance to anything going on in your life at the time. When this happens, don't resist it. God knows that it's a verse you'll need in the future. Think of it as being similar to storing extra food in your freezer or pantry. When you need to prepare a meal quickly or unexpectedly, you already have what you need to make it work. Now, back to Kim.

I already knew the exact scripture that applied to Kim's situation and had been meditating on this particular verse—or *making it my truth*—even before I misplaced my keys. When I told her to say, "Thank you, God, for leading me to the truth of where my cell phone is located," every time she thought about her keys, she didn't know that she was *lifespeaking*. She didn't know that she was speaking life based on scripture . . . but I knew!

And because she trusted me as her friend, she had confidence that I wouldn't steer her wrong. She had faith in my words, but my words were based on God's Word. So, my faith was already locked, loaded, and ready to work. Once she made those promises, I grabbed her by the hand and told her this: "Now, we're going to pray because God cares about what you care about. Since you care about your cell phone, He cares about it, too. Let's get His help to find it!"

Let me explain something here. My holding Kim's hand to pray is symbolic of me joining my faith with hers. This reminds me of one time when Kim was trying to move a bed from one room of her home into another. She thought she could do it by herself. But, when she realized that she was trapped in one room, with the bed stuck in the doorway, she called me to come over and help. Together, we were able to move the bed where she wanted it to be. In this instance, Kim was stuck again. She just couldn't find her phone and needed my help or, in this case, my faith to get the job done. Let's continue.

So, with the enthusiastic innocence and faith of a child, Kim closed her eyes and bowed her head as we held hands right there in the backyard on a warm sunny day with our four young children laughing, playing, and running around. My prayer that day went something like this:

Father, God, thank you that Your Word is truth. We can trust it, depend on it, and know that You'll make it good. Now, Father, Your Word says in John 16:13 that, 'When He, the Spirit of truth, has come, He will guide you into all truth.' So, God, in accordance with that word, we ask that You lead and guide Kim to the truth of where her cell phone is located. We know that You care about what Kim cares about, and since You will lead Kim to her phone, we thank You that she won't even have to look for it. So, now, we receive it, we thank You for it, and we call it 'done' in Jesus' name, Amen!

Kim looked up and said, "Amen!"

I followed the prayer with a few more instructions. I told Kim, "Do not look for your phone. We asked God to *guide* you to it. So, stop thinking about it and let the Word do the work." She agreed.

This is an abbreviated version of the process because some of the steps had already been taken on Kim's behalf. (Again, that's why it's great to have people in your life who can pray with you and for you. When they pray for you, the Bible refers to that as intercession or standing in the gap. That's when you pray with or for someone who cannot, for whatever reason, pray for themselves). However, the steps and the process were the same. Let's take a look:

1. **Watch your words.** Kim had to stop agreeing with what she didn't want.

2. **Find the truth.** I'd already found a scripture that I had recently meditated on.

3. **Make it yours.** I had been meditating on that verse for some time, so I already had faith in it. I had no doubt that it was going to work for us.

4. **LifeSpeak and win!** That thing I told Kim to say every time she thought about her cell phone? That was Kim lifespeaking. She was speaking life (God's Word) to her situation. All she had to do was to stick with it to get the win.

Kim did exactly as she had promised. Every time she thought of her cell phone or was tempted to start looking for it, she would stop and say, "God, thank you for guiding me to the truth of where my cell phone is located." For the next three days, or so I thought, Kim resisted the temptation to look for her phone. She resisted the temptation to say, "It was missing." She stopped saying she couldn't find it. She even refused to go buy a new one. But, days later . . .

Kim and I were at the bus stop with the kids one morning, three or four days later, and, honestly, I had totally forgotten all about the whole thing when she looked at me with a big grin on her face and said, "Oh, yeah! I forgot to tell you . . . I found my phone! I found it the very next day, too! And I never even looked for it. Not even once. I was actually on the house phone when I turned and looked at the pantry because I'd left the door open. When I went over to close it, I looked up, not even thinking about my cell phone, and saw it sitting on one of the shelves on top of a can. Then I remembered that I'd put it there to keep Mikey [her toddler] from playing with it. So, thank you so much for that prayer. It worked!"

I turned to her and reminded her of the bigger picture. "Kim," I said in my serious, real-talk voice, "if God cares about your cell phone, how much more does He care about your family, your job, your health, or all the other really big things in your life?" Kim's eyes filled with tears. She nodded in agreement as I added, "See, the faith is the same. The process is the same. God is looking for someone who will believe His Word, speak His Word, and do His Word." That's what I said to Kim. Now, I'm speaking to you:

It doesn't matter if your concern is a big issue or a small one. God cares about a cell phone, and He cares about a loved one that is dealing with an addiction. He cares as much about a sick child as he cares about your child having playmates. He cares about your personal health, your marriage, and maybe something you desire but think that you don't deserve. He cares about everything we care about. *Everything we care about—Everything.*

In I Peter 5:6-7, it says, "Therefore humble yourselves under the mighty hand of God, that He may exalt you in due time, casting all of your care upon Him, for He cares for you." God cares about what you care about. Your concerns are His, so take the time to:

1. **Watch your words** and stop agreeing with the things (in your life) that you don't desire.

2. **Find the truth** in scripture (and translation) that addresses your concern.

3. **Make it yours.** Make it your truth by meditating on that scripture until it brings faith, until you believe in the truth more than you believe the facts.

4. **Lifespeak until you win**—yes, lifespeak . . .

   • **about it** – that's speaking God's Word *about* your situation

   • **to it** – that's speaking God's Word *to* your situation

   • **through it** – that's speaking God's Word even as you're going *through* your situation

When you lifespeak *about it, to it, and through it,* whatever challenge you're facing will have to change. Your situation will have to conform to the words you're speaking. You will take those unwanted facts and watch them bow to the truth of your Word-of-God-based desired result. This is how we *lifespeak and win!*

CHAPTER FIVE

Joe's Story

My friend Ashley received terrible news: Her husband, Joe, was diagnosed with cancer. As alarming as the news had been to her, she knew that the Word of God was stronger than any diagnosis. Ashley was no rookie Christian. She had been through some tough times before and watched as God provided the miracles and answers she needed. He did it then, so this truster-in-God's Word believed He would do it again. This time, she was counting on God to come through for her *and* Joe.

Ashley went into combat mode. Refusing to waste time, she contacted a small circle of friends, who she could rely on, to stand with her and her family in prayer. Ashley was ready to go into this battle and come out with a win. Let's review the steps and see how Ashley and Joe applied them to win:

1. **Watch your words**. Ashley had to watch her words. She could not agree with the doctor's diagnosis, so she never called it, "Joe's cancer." Joe didn't want it. She didn't want it. So, they never agreed with the cancer they didn't want.

If you went to a restaurant and ordered a fruit salad, and the server brought you a plate of raw onions, would you just accept it? Would you just take the onions and eat them? No! Of course, not! Do you know what you'd do? You'd send that plate back! You'd say, "That's not what I ordered." Then, you would send it back. Well, Ashley and Joe didn't order cancer! They didn't want cancer! And they were not going to accept cancer! Ashley and Joe knew they had a right to reject cancer! They were determined to send cancer back!

2. **Find the truth.** They searched the scriptures to find the truth. They even had friends come over and conduct Bible studies in their home on the subject of healing to keep their faith firmly rooted and established in the power of God's Word. Listen, folks, the enemy plays for keeps. You can speak life to your life, or you can speak death to your life. Well, someone had spoken cancer to Joe's life, and He was not having it.

Please note: We thank God for good doctors because, without their care and expertise, most of the population wouldn't stand a chance to maintain their health. Not everyone knows how to walk by faith. So, I am not showing any disrespect to doctors. I have a doctor, and I love my doctor. I need to get this truth on record. Also, I am not endorsing prayer for healing as a substitute for healthy habits. You should eat well, get enough sleep, and exercise in accordance with your physician's recommendations. We should not knowingly abuse our bodies and then count on prayer and lifespeaking as a way to mitigate the impact or damage that our reckless behaviors can cause.

Ashley and Joe searched the Word of God to find the truth that addressed their circumstances. The scripture that resonated with them was Isaiah 53:5 KJV. They found the truth, scripture, and translation.

3. **Make it yours.** How do you make the truth your truth? How do you make that verse or scripture yours? How do you take ownership of the truth?

You own your truth through meditation. Meditation is how we get our subconscious to absorb the truth. It's how the truth becomes more real than the unwanted facts. They meditated on that scripture together. Not just Ashley and Joe, but their children and friends as well. The entire family and their community of friends were standing in faith, believing in God for Joe's healing.

4. **LifeSpeak and win!** Lifepeaking is best described as taking
   the truth of God's Word that you've meditated on and made
   your own and then combining it with a declaration to address an unwanted fact in your life until that fact conforms
   to the truth. One way to say this is that you're speaking the
   words from a script you created from the scripture. Then
   you speak it out or declare it no matter what happens, how
   things look, how you feel, or what people say. Ashley and
   Joe kept it simple. Whenever anyone asked about Joe, they
   would lifespeak by saying, "By Jesus' stripes, Joe is healed. In
   Jesus' name." Notice that they said, "Joe *is* healed," not "Joe
   will be healed." That's because faith is *now*. Hebrews 11:1
   says, "Now, faith is the substance of things hoped for, the
   evidence of things not seen." See, faith is *now*.

They were lifespeaking. Not just Ashley, Joe, and the kids, but their
extended family and friends as well! We were all declaring, "By Jesus'
stripes, Joe is healed." Do you see it? Lifespeaking is taking the truth
of the Word of God that you've meditated on and made your own and
declaring it (and only it) regarding your circumstances. You're using
the power of the truth to make the unwanted facts of your life bow in
submission. God's Word is stronger than any diagnosis. The truth is
stronger than the facts. Life is more powerful than death. This is how
we fight our battles. This is fighting the good fight of faith.

The next months were filled with doctor appointments, chemotherapy treatments, prayer, and lifespeaking. As they continued to follow
the doctors' instructions, they also continued to lifespeak and believe
God's Word. They knew that the truth of God's Word was more powerful than the facts of cancer.

Beware: This isn't a game. This is life or death. And the symptoms
come to test your faith, your resolve, and your endurance. Don't let
the symptoms fool you into stepping back and loosening your grip on
God's Word. Ashley and Joe didn't. Were they challenged? Yes! Was
their battle a cakewalk? No way! But they knew they couldn't back
down. They had to have the tenacity of a pit bull and refuse to say

anything that didn't agree with what they were declaring. So when Joe:

- had no appetite, they said, "By Jesus' stripes, Joe *is* healed!"

- lost a lot of weight, they said, "By Jesus' stripes, Joe *is* healed!"

- was seriously fatigued, they said, "By Jesus' stripes, Joe *is* healed!"

- was yellowed from the chemotherapy, they said, "By Jesus' stripes, Joe *is* healed!"

- was weakened from the meds and could barely speak for himself, Ashley declared for him, "By Jesus' stripes, Joe *is* healed!"

Since this is a "How-To" book, let's take the time to highlight the present tense of their words again: They spoke in the present tense, not the future tense. Healing was not *going* to happen for Joe. Healing was *already an established truth* based on God's Word. So, they didn't say, "Joe is going to be healed." They said, "Joe *is* healed." They understood that the truth of God's Word is *now*. God's Word is true *right now*. Do you see that? Joe and Ashley continued to speak that truth, fully determined to see the truth make the facts bow. And, in spite of the physical evidence that Joe's condition seemed to grow worse, they were never deterred. Instead, they kept on lifespeaking. They understood Joe's physical condition could not outlast the power of God's Word as long as they held on to it.

Galatians 6:9 (NIV) says, "Let us not become weary in doing good, for at the proper time we will reap a harvest if we do not give up." What was the good that Ashley, Joe, and their family and friends were doing? Lifespeaking! They continued to speak life into a near-death-looking health crisis. They didn't get weary. They didn't cave in. They didn't quit. They stayed focused on the truth of God's Word. Joe's physical condition was a fact. It was a fact that couldn't bully them. And it couldn't intimidate the truth they were lifespeaking. And here's the thing about facts: They are temporary, which means they are subject to change. So, Ashley and Joe ignored the facts and focused on the truth. Take a look at how the Apostle Paul explained it in II Corinthians 4:17-18:

For our light affliction, which is but for a moment, worketh for us a far more exceeding and eternal weight of glory; While we look not at the things which are seen [in this case, the facts, the test results, the medical diagnosis, Joe's symptoms, etc.], but the things which are not seen [the truth, the power of God's Word working in Joe's body, the faith they had in God's Word], for the things which are seen are temporal [or subject to change; has a limited time; is passing]; but the things which are not seen are eternal [lasting, never-changing, forever like the truth of God's Word].

So, what happened?

After weeks and months of meds, prayer, chemo, lifespeaking, specialized dietary recommendations, lifespeaking, doctor appointments, hair loss, weight loss, lifespeaking ... something began to change. Joe began to grow stronger. The doctors began to see improvements in his test results. What was happening? The truth of God's Word that Joe and Ashley held on to, that they kept speaking, that they kept declaring in the face of so much contradiction . . . that truth outlasted the facts. The facts were bowing down to the truth! Eventually, the facts did bow to the truth, completely, and Joe was declared *cancer-free* by his doctors! Joe is alive and healthy to this day.

Now, the question is: Why doesn't everyone do this? Well, some people don't do this because they don't know this. Sometimes, they start on this path, but the symptoms begin to intimidate them, and they give up. Lifespeaking works! Lifespeaking works because it's backed by the Word of God. Lifespeaking works because it changes the unwanted facts to match the truth of God's Word. In this case, the unwanted fact was cancer, but lifespeaking—taking that live and active power of God's Word that you've meditated on so that it is alive and active in your life—will work for you, no matter what the situation. God's Word, the truth, will always cause the facts to bow. But you have to fight the good fight of faith. You have to keep that word coming out of your mouth.

You'll have to declare God's Word no matter how it looks, no matter how you feel, and no matter what everyone else is saying. Let me warn you: If you choose to take this path to victory, you'll probably experience times when you look ridiculous. Some of your friends and relatives may call you crazy. They may say you are "in denial." But listen, if looking ridiculous or being called crazy is the price you have to pay for your healing, for your deliverance, or for your victory, or to save the life of someone you love, then that's a price you should be more than willing to pay! This is how you lifespeak, folks. This is how you speak life to your life . . . and win!

CHAPTER SIX

My Story

One of the most challenging days of my life as a parent happened when my youngest daughter was about nine years old. She had been wearing braces for about six months at the time.

On this particular day, we were just getting home but had plans to attend a family event later that evening. As we pulled into the garage, my daughter asked if she could ride her scooter until it was time for us to leave again. It was a reasonable request, so I consented and went inside as she ran towards her scooter and helmet. It was almost 4 pm. She had been riding her scooter happily for about ten minutes when she hit an uneven section of sidewalk. Her speed, combined with the impact, knocked her helmet off and caused her to fall, face down, mouth opened, onto the concrete.

Somehow, she managed to walk home crying, bleeding, and unaware of the severity of her injuries. When she got to the house and started banging on the door, one of my teenage daughters answered. When my teenage daughter saw her little sister's face, she started screaming and crying. All the commotion sent me running to the door to find out what was happening. When I reached the two of them, all I could see was blood dripping from my nine-year-old daughter's mouth and her front teeth dangling by her gums, along with the twisted metal of her braces. It was by the grace of God that I didn't allow myself to examine the damage closely, as it was clear that it was extensive. But, for some reason (and this had to be God, too), I grabbed a bath towel from the nearby restroom and wrapped it around her entire head with a circular motion. With the towel wrapped to cover her mouth, I pushed upwards, and to this day, I don't know why I did that. Maybe it was a subconscious attempt (I'm not even sure) to push her front teeth back up *into* the gum sockets, but then, I rushed to start making calls for help.

My first call was to her orthodontist, Dr. Bomeli. When I called "Dr. B's" office, I was told via a recording that the office was closed. Fortunately, Dr. Bomeli had given us his cell number, and when I called, he graciously agreed to meet us at his office. When my little girl and I got there, Dr. B was literally turning on all the lights in the office in preparation for our arrival. We walked over to one of the dental chairs and waited for him. When my daughter reclined in the dental chair, Dr. B removed the towel from around her head and uncovered her mouth. It was obvious: he was in shock. After he regained his calm and tried to remain professional, he explained to me that she needed to get X-rays taken at our dentist's office, but before that could even happen, there was work that he needed to perform. The trauma was so severe that the orthodontist had to stabilize her teeth before she could even get X-rays taken to assess the scope of the damage.

As Dr. B examined the impact of the trauma to determine where and how to begin, it was clear that he desperately needed a dental assistant. Since Dr. B couldn't reach for his instruments and actually tend to her mouth at the same time, I became the "acting" dental assistant. What a motley crew we were: My daughter, bloodied, bruised, and with extensive oral injuries, lying face up, mouth open in that big dental chair; Dr. B, so challenged by this trauma that we both knew he was "winging it"; and me, still running on adrenaline but also finding myself having to assist Dr. B, even though I didn't have a clue about any of the instruments on the table before me. None of that mattered. We had to work together to help my little girl.

This is how we proceeded: Dr. B would ask for an instrument, and I'd pick one up and say, "This one?" to which he would reply, "No, not that one. The other one." I would pick up something else, show it to him, and say, "This one?" And he would say, "No, the one to the right of it." We kept repeating this process until I got it right, and we did it all over again whenever he required a different dental tool. It took almost three hours for him to get her teeth in stable enough condition for her to be able to get X-rays taken by our family dentist. (Side note: The trauma to my daughter's mouth and teeth was so severe that, months later, Dr. B returned to school to take additional classes on how to stabilize teeth in cases of trauma.)

Once her teeth were stabilized, we left Dr. B's office and headed to the office of our family's dentist. Thankfully, Dr. B had called ahead, explained the details of the accident, and given the dentist an idea of what to expect from my daughter's injuries.

When we arrived at around 7 pm, we were told that our family dentist was on vacation, but another dentist on staff would take care of us. Thankfully, this happened on a day when the dentist's office was opened late. The staff dentist took a look at my daughter's mouth and told us he was amazed by the job Dr. B had done in stabilizing our daughter's teeth. This gave us hope. (Little did we know that his comments about Dr. B's work would be the only positive thing we'd hear from him that night.) Then, he took a series of X-rays and reviewed them. After that, the dentist on staff didn't provide a single ounce of good news. He didn't even try. The minute he opened his mouth, we could tell it was all going to be doom and gloom.

He began by telling us about his credentials. I believe he did this to establish his expertise. He wanted us to accept his words without question. Then, he gave us a laundry list of complications that he believed my daughter would suffer from in the future as a result of the accident. He said she'd experience severe headaches, she would need a root canal and possibly implants, and that she would suffer from sensitive gums for the rest of her life.

Now, my nine-year-old daughter was sitting there, listening, as this dentist continued to decry the future of her oral health. His every word was like a brushstroke painting a bleaker and bleaker picture. I had to do something. I had to say something, right there, at that moment, so that my little girl would know that this man, while he had good intentions, would not get the final word about her oral health. So, what did I do?

Every time he'd say something negative, I'd say, "It appears that way to you?" or "That's what you think?" or "You believe so?" Eventually, he got angry with my responses and said, "Listen, Mrs. Hollis. I've been a dentist for 'X' amount of years." (I don't actually remember the exact number he said, but I do remember that the number was high enough to be impressive.) He continued, "I know what I'm talking about. Now, I'm trying to prepare you for what's in store for your daughter in the future." While I never agreed with his words, I thanked him for his time, effort, and expertise as we left the office.

So, my baby girl, who was thrown off her scooter and face planted, with helmet off and mouth opened, onto the concrete, was in pain, bruised, scarred, and now, thanks to the relentless negative prognosis of the dentist, probably very scared. We'd spent about three hours with the orthodontist and another three hours at the dentist.

She was still wearing the same shirt and carrying the bath towel I had wrapped around her head—both had bloodstains everywhere. Her lips were swollen, and her face, nose, and arms were all covered with bloodied scratches. It was pretty dark now, and as we walked to the car, I knew I had to speak words of light and life to cancel all that darkness that the dentist had spoken over her.

Yes, she was tired. Yes, she was hungry. Yes, she was only nine years old. It had been a long, hard day, but remember, this is when the fight of faith begins.

All I wanted to do was get my baby girl home, cleaned up, and tucked into bed. But I had a job to do first. See, I couldn't leave the staff dentist's negative words out there, unanswered and unchecked, to allow them to play over and over in my daughter's head. I had to stop those words from harassing her before they started. I had to say something. I had to let my daughter know that God's Word would be the final authority in this situation . . . not what that dentist had said.

When we got in the car, she sat in the back seat to stretch out. I turned toward her from the driver's seat and said, "Sweetie, I know you're tired. You took a really, really hard fall. And I know that the dentist said a lot of stuff and . . . none of it was very good. Now, let me tell you the facts. Your lips and face are still pretty swollen. You have scrapes and scratches all over your face. I'm sure you're still in pain. Now, those are the facts. But God's Word says, 'By the stripes of Jesus, you are healed.' So, although you look like you've been in a fight with an angry cat and lost [she half-smiled at that], the Bible says, 'You are healed.' It doesn't say, 'You are going to be healed.' It says, 'You *are* healed.' Got it? So, we are going to pray, okay? And we are not going to receive or agree with any of the bad news that the dentist just spoke. We are going to pray and declare that when we come back here for your follow-up appointment, there will be *no trace* that you ever even had an accident. Okay? Do you agree with me on that?"

She nodded in agreement, and then we held hands, prayed, and declared everything we had just discussed. With that, I turned forward, started the car, and we headed home. Then, my baby girl started humming a song I wrote and taught her months before called "I believe I'm healed."

The song says, "I believe I'm healed. I believe I'm healed. I am standing on God's promises and not on how I feel. That is why. That is why I believe I'm healed."

She hummed that song until she fell asleep. Once I was sure that she was sleeping soundly, I cried the rest of the way home.

For the next few weeks, we moved from super-soft foods, including baby food, to soft, room-temperature foods, to progressively firmer foods. The first time she had fries again, although they were room temperature, was a real treat.

Every day, we continued to declare that there would be *no trace* that the accident ever occurred. Based on what happened and the extent of the damage, we would have sounded ridiculous to the average person. It looked impossible, but we held firm to our faith. We stayed focused on the truth, not the facts. We kept declaring the truth of God's Word and kept disagreeing with the facts of the damage caused by the accident.

About six months later, I took my daughter back to the dentist for her first follow-up, a check-up with the intent of getting approval from our family dentist for Dr. B to continue the protocol for braces. This time, our family dentist was in the office.

She greeted us by saying she'd been told all about the accident and had reviewed the X-rays that were taken on that day. As she prepared our daughter for new X-rays, she said, "Let's see where things are now." She took a series of X-rays of my daughter's mouth and teeth, and then she asked us to go back to the waiting room while she reviewed the information. As my daughter and I waited to hear the results, our dentist walked into the room looking confused and perplexed. When she finally spoke, she said, "This is remarkable! I looked at her X-rays, and there is no trace that she ever suffered any trauma."

Did you read that? Our dentist actually used the words "no trace." She used the exact words we had declared as we sat in the car and prayed on the evening of the accident after the more-than-six-hour ordeal. No trace! I wish you could have seen the expressions on our faces as we turned to one another at the sound of the words "no trace." I wish I could have seen our faces. How exactly did this happen?

Listed below are some of the scripture references that will help explain how and why we use the Word of God to make facts change to the truth.

Job 22:28 - *You will also decree a thing, and it will be established for you; And light will shine upon your ways.*

We made a decree—or declaration—that there would be no trace. And the decree we made was established. Do you see it?

Proverbs 18:21 - *Death and life are in the power of the tongue, and those who love it will eat its fruit.*

We spoke life with the power of our tongues. No matter how much baby food my daughter had to eat, how swollen her face was, how many scratches she had, we spoke life, and we received the fruit (result) of no trace of the accident for her life.

Ephesians 5:1 - *Therefore be imitators of God as dear children.*

We imitated God. See, we are to imitate God the same way children imitate their mothers and fathers. While this verse speaks specifically regarding love, it applies to all things. We are to imitate God in all things. And that's what we were doing; by decreeing the outcome, speaking life, etc., we imitated God.

Romans 4:17b - *God, who gives life to the dead and calls those things which do not exist as though they did.*

We called those things that did not exist as if they did. We called her "healed" (past tense). We declared "no trace." We called those things out even before they became visible to our physical eyes. We imitated God.

John 15:7 - *If you abide in Me, and My words abide in you, you will ask what you desire, and it shall be done for you.*

Remember the instances in your life where there was no time to stop and meditate on the Word? Well, because I meditated on the Word, the truth was already abiding within me, so I could use my faith on behalf of whoever's unwanted fact needed to be changed to the truth. See, that's the importance of meditation. It's how you keep the Word abiding in you. And this verse says that if the Word is abiding in you, whatever you ask, it will be done for you. See, this is how you take ownership of the truth and make it work for you.

Joshua 1:8-9 - *This Book of the Law shall not depart from your mouth, but you shall meditate on it day and night, that you may observe to do according to all that is written in it. For then you will make your way prosperous, and then you will have good success. Have I not commanded you? Be strong and of good courage; do* *not be afraid, nor be dismayed, for the Lord your God is with you wherever you go.*

This verse is talking about meditating on God's Word as a lifestyle— that's what is meant by "day and night." When you meditate on God's Word on a regular basis, it keeps you ready for the storms of life. When the rain comes, you have the umbrella of God's Word ready to shield you as you lifespeak your way to victory.

Matthew 12:37 - *For by your words you will be justified, and by your words you will be condemned.*

We had a choice to make: Our words could justify my daughter and bring healing, or they could condemn her and bring agreement with the staff dentist and his negative prognosis. We had to make a choice. We chose to decree "no trace." We chose to speak life. We chose to call those things we desired. We chose to be justified. We chose to *lifespeak!*

In the face of the trauma and the negative prognosis of the dentist, we stood firm. In the face of sheer contradiction, we had the righteous audacity to *lifespeak*. How did we do it? Let's recap:

HOW DID WE LIFESPEAK AND WIN?

We did the same thing you will have to do. Remember the steps?

1. **Watch your words.** We didn't agree with the things that we didn't desire. We only spoke life-giving words. Only!

2. **Find the truth.** We knew scriptures that addressed our concern (the dentist's prognosis).

3. **Make it yours.** We made the truth our truth by meditating on the scriptures. In this case, my entire family had meditated on Isaiah 53:5, Job 22:28, and Romans 4:17 and already had faith in them. We believed those verses more than we believed the words of the dentist. They were our truth!

4. **LifeSpeak and win!** We made a faith-filled declaration about the outcome of the injuries that my daughter had suffered,

"By Jesus' stripes, you are healed, and there will be no trace that the accident ever happened" (based on Isaiah 53:5, Job 22:28, and Romans 4:17). Then, we had to lifespeak that declaration all the way to victory!

We had to lifespeak . . .

- **about it** – that's speaking God's Word *about* your situation.

- **to it** – that's speaking God's Word *to* your situation.

- **through it** – that's speaking God's Word as you're going *through* your situation.

Now, some of you may be wondering, "How long do you lifespeak?" My answer is this: You lifespeak for as long as it takes for the victory you have on the inside of you to show up on the outside. You lifespeak until the image of victory that's in your heart shows up in your house, or on your body, at your job, or on your doorstep, in your bank account, or in your marriage, wherever it's supposed to be. You lifespeak until everyone who didn't believe can see your win with their own eyes. Romans 4:17 says that "God calls those things that be not as though they were." We kept calling my daughter's condition "no trace" until our family dentist, and everyone else saw that there was no trace. So you just keep calling those things that be not. For how long? Until they are! So again, you keep lifespeaking for as long as it takes for everyone to see what you're saying. You keep speaking life with those faith-filled words and watch victory show up every time. How do you know you'll win every time? Let me show you by providing Isaiah 55:11 in the following three translations:

So shall my word be that goeth forth out of my mouth: it shall not return to me void, but it shall accomplish that which I please, and it shall prosper in the thing whereto I sent it. (KJV- King James Version)

So shall My word be that goes out of my mouth: it shall not return to Me void (without producing any effect, useless), but it shall accomplish that which I please and purpose, and it shall prosper in the thing for which I sent it. (AMP - The Amplified Bible)

So will the words that come out of my mouth not come back empty-handed. They'll do the work that I sent them to do, they'll complete the assignment I gave them. (MSG - The Message Bible)

Do you see that? Remember what we read in Ephesians 5:1? That we are to "be imitators of God as dear children." This is telling us that, according to Isaiah 55:11, when we do what our Father does, when we imitate Him by speaking His Word, we will get His results. We have His promise, His truth that His Word will never come back void, unproductive, useless, or empty-handed. As we keep lifespeaking, God has guaranteed us that we will win!

Are you wondering how my daughter is doing now? Here's the update:

My daughter was nine years old when she had that scooter accident. As of this writing, she just graduated from high school, and she has never, I repeat, *never* had severe headaches, gum sensitivity, dental surgeries, implants, or any of the other complications that the dentist predicted would be the aftermath of her injuries. *Never.* There is still, to this day, *no trace* that she ever suffered any trauma at all to her mouth, teeth, or gums. *No trace!*

This is why we lifespeak. This is how we lifespeak. This is how we take the unwanted facts of our lives and change them to reflect the glorious truth of God's Word.

You have the power, the choice, and the right to be a lifespeaker. You have the power to take on the current, undesirable facts of your life and make them bow to the truth of God's Word. C'mon, folks! It's time for us to lifespeak. It's time for all of us to speak life to our lives and win! So the question now is: What will you do? It's your turn. The ball is in your court. I am challenging you to take what you've learned and get moving. You have everything you need to get going right now.

But, before we part ways, I've got one more, very personal, story to share . . .

CHAPTER SEVEN

My Story Continues: Mother/Daughter Anxiety Battle

On August 29, the Thursday right before the Labor Day holiday weekend of 2019, my oldest daughter and I were on our way to pick up my youngest daughter from college. The following is my Instagram account of what happened during that drive:

It happened in a split second.

My daughter and I were driving on the expressway when an 18-wheeler pulled into the far-left lane (where we were driving between 70-75 mph) and cut us off. Then, without warning, the truck made a quick swerve. After that, a wide, mangled piece of metal rolled from under the truck right toward us, crashing into the front of our SUV. Some of the metal rolled under the car and got lodged underneath. Suddenly, the car was getting hot. We needed to get out . . . fast!

By God's grace, we were able to quickly cross four lanes of speeding traffic and pull over to the far-right lane (it was as if all the cars started moving in slow motion for a few minutes just so we could get over), and we jumped out of the vehicle!

Meanwhile, cars, trucks, and RVs were whizzing by at 70-80 mph. The car was smoking, oil was leaking, and we are running alongside the expressway to get away from the car. (Lord, please don't let the car blow up).

Thankfully, we both had our phones and began making calls for help.

We are so grateful for Highway Safety Patrol, EMTs, Fire & Rescue, and AAA, but we are most thankful to God for his mercy and protection.

I was able to call home and tell everyone that we were safe. It could have ended differently. See, the truth is, we are all, every one of us, one phone call from our knees.

It happened in a split second.

That was a post from my Instagram account. What followed was something that neither I nor my daughter, who was driving at the time of the incident, had anticipated. Both of us began to experience panic attacks whenever we had to drive or ride in a car on the expressway.

For the first couple of weeks after the accident, everyone seemed to be okay. We weren't physically or visibly injured, and, frankly, we were just thankful to be alive. But, after a few weeks, something began happening to each of us that neither of us mentioned to anyone, not even to each other.

My daughter and I were both fighting a battle that was slowly crippling us emotionally. It was anxiety. I was completely unaware of the challenges she was having with anxiety, and she was completely unaware of mine. I think we both tried to ignore it at first, only to discover that the problem was getting progressively worse.

Then, something happened that forced me to face it. Almost three weeks after the accident, I was in the car with my husband, riding on the passenger's side. As a truck began to merge into our lane, I began contorting my body away from the truck as if it was an effort to physically avoid a collision with the truck. Not only that, but I also began making sounds—almost whimpering noises—in an effort to suppress a desire to scream and alert my husband to the intense internal struggle I was having.

The truck merged in front of us without incident, but when the lane switch was over and I felt fairly safe again, I had this incredible urge to cry. I mean, really, really cry.

My husband didn't say anything at first. For weeks, he had been aware of my struggle because of the wincing sounds and physical reactions I had made while riding in the car with him. I didn't realize how obvious they were, and he was waiting for me to say something to him.

Finally, I had to face it. I couldn't live like this. I wouldn't allow my daughter to live like this. I had to do something. Pray? Of course! But, in addition to prayer, I knew I had to get rid of the "every time I am in a car on the expressway, I am afraid I will have an accident" seeds that were planted in my mind during that Labor Day weekend incident.

So, what did I do? I had to recognize and confront the anxiety as a fact . . . an unwanted fact. If you are dealing with anxiety, you have to recognize it as a fact, too. We can't "not mention it" away. We can't pretend it's not there. We cannot conquer what we won't confront. Anxiety under those particular circumstances of riding on the passenger's side of a car on the expressway had become a fact, specifically around trucks. That's what it was: A fact. It was an unwelcomed, unwanted fact. But still a fact. However, the good news was that I knew that to change an unwanted fact, all I needed was a God-backed truth. So, I had to find the truth I needed to win; I needed to get my life back and feel safe again whenever I rode in a car on the expressway. Where would I go to find that truth? John 17:17 says, "Thy Word is truth." I had to search God's Word to find the truth I needed to turn this anxiety thing from a loss into a win. On September 29, 2019, this was the verse I found that resonated with me and that I used to address the challenges I was having with anxiety:

Don't worry about anything; instead, pray about everything. Tell God what you need and thank him for all he has done. Then you will experience God's peace, which exceeds anything we can understand. His peace will guard your hearts and minds as you live in Christ Jesus. (Philippians 4:7)

The process of finding this verse was like mining for gold. I knew that there was a remedy for the anxiety because it didn't come from God. How do I know that? Because God is good, and a good Father would never give his child anxiety attacks. His Word says that He'll keep us in perfect peace: "You will keep in perfect peace those whose minds are steadfast, because they trust you" (Isaiah 26:3 NIV). God is not the author of confusion. He wouldn't promise perfect peace if it was His will for us to have anxiety. This was the hidden treasure. This was the key to my puzzle, the answer to my prayer, the truth that was going to make the unwanted fact called "anxiety" bow to God's Word. It was the truth that I was going to use, to meditate on, to speak in faith. This was the truth that was going to set me FREE! (Read John 8:32 NIV.) So, I took the steps:

1. **Watch your words.** I never called it my anxiety. Now, was it anxiety? Yes, definitely, but it wasn't mine. I didn't want it. I didn't ask for it. It didn't come from God. So, I didn't agree with what I didn't want. My mission: Send it back.

2. **Find the truth.** I found the truth that addressed the issue (anxiety). See, peace is the opposite of anxiety. The power of the peace of God can make the fact of anxiety bow.

3. **Make it yours.** I made the truth mine. I took ownership of that truth by meditating on that verse until the reality of the truth of God's peace became more real than the unwanted fact of anxiety. I made it my truth. I took possession of that truth. Yes, I meditated on the Word until faith came and until I believed in the truth more than I believed in the fact of anxiety. Now, did anxiety exist? Again, yes. But it no longer had the power, or the right, to live inside or harass me.

4. **LifeSpeak and win!** Once faith came, I was ready to lifespeak. I was ready to speak the life of God's Word with the power to change my circumstances. I was ready to declare my freedom from anxiety because I had faith in God's Word. I didn't focus on anxiety (why would I focus on something I didn't want?). Instead, I focused on God's peace.

So, what did I do? I followed the steps. This isn't magic; this is faith, and because I only felt this anxiety when riding in the car as a passenger, it was easy to measure how my faith was growing. It was easy to check my progress.

Listen, I am going to be completely transparent here because it's the only way I can really help you. At one point, I was meditating and meditating on that verse. Then, I thought, "Okay, okay, I got this. I'm ready." And, really, I thought I was. I thought it was settled.

The reality hit me, however, the next time I got in the car. I don't even remember where I was going, but I was only thinking about reaching my destination. I wasn't thinking about having an anxiety attack on the way. Every time I rode in the car as a passenger and the drive required us to get on the expressway, I would be totally fine. I was fine, that is until a truck came near us.

Whenever I saw a truck, there would be a heightened sense of awareness. I found myself trying to "help" the driver, no matter who it was, drive more carefully. I would check the mirrors, check the speed, and ask questions like, "Do you see that truck?" or "Maybe you should slow down and let them go wherever they want to go." Then, as I realized what I was doing—co-driving and worrying and commenting and advising and making those anti-trusting-God-with- high-anxiety moves—I realized I needed to go "back to the drawing board" and start my meditation process all over again. My faith wasn't strong enough yet. You can handle my transparency, right? Notice, I said, "yet."

God's Word always works. Always. As long as you don't give up, cave in, or quit, God's Word will do the job. So, whenever it seems that God's Word isn't producing the promised outcome, guess what? It's not the Word. It's the "you." Or, in this case, it was the "me." Yep, it was me. Listen, I wasn't doing it wrong, as far as the meditation was concerned. I just had to keep doing more of what I was doing. So, I needed to go back and spend more time with the Word. Period.

Think of it this way: When you're learning to ride a bike, and you fall off multiple times, you don't say that it's the bike's fault, do you?

No, of course not! You recognize that you have to go back and try it again, and again, and maybe a few more times. You were probably motivated by the thought that you had to learn so you could go bike riding with all your friends. You didn't want to be left out, right?

You have to put in more effort and time and make a deeper commitment. When it comes to learning how to ride a bike, you have to master the skill of balance to the degree that it overcomes the law of gravity.

In my case, my faith had to get strong enough, and I had to meditate on the Word intently enough so that its truth would overcome the facts. Want to know what motivated me? It was knowing that peace belonged to me and that anxiety was trying to steal it away from me, and that made me angry. Thinking this way gave me a greater determination to work God's Word to its fullest potential. It should give you that same determination in your life, not just with anxiety (that was my case), but in any area of your life that is being taunted by an unwanted fact.

So, I dug in deeper. I stood stronger. I meditated longer. I increased the intensity. I had to up my game. And I did!

The car incident happened in September of 2019. I meditated on the Word for months. Sometimes, a ride on the expressway would catch me off-guard, and I would find myself jumping and feeling panic and anxiety again. Each time, my reaction would let me know that I had to continue meditating on the Word. I knew that God's Word was true; I just had to keep meditating on it. Some days, the ride would go well. Other days, not so much. But I kept meditating. I began checking my confidence with every trip on the expressway. Then, in February 2020, my husband and I planned a six-hour road trip. There would be no "not-thinking" about testing my faith level this time. This was going to be my opportunity to gauge whether or not I'd finally received the victory that God had waiting for me. I was about to take a six-hour faith exam. Here's what happened:

On Friday morning, February 7, 2020, my husband and I began the six-hour road trip that would serve as a test of my victory over anxiety.

Interestingly, one of my "instadaughters" (daughters from Instagram) had sent me two worship songs earlier that week that had been ministering to me for days. One of the songs, entitled "Bow Down and Worship," had been on my heart from the moment I heard it. While I believed I was ready to handle the trip, you don't really know until you know. The first thirty minutes of the trip went well. And then, and I am not exaggerating, I noticed what appeared to be a fleet of FedEx trucks up ahead of us. These were not regular 18-wheeler trucks; no, these were trucks that were connected in tandem. I had never, in my life, seen so many trucks on the highway at one time. Listen, these were multiple trucks that had three trailers hitched together! When I realized what we were driving toward, my thought was, "Are you kidding me?" I almost couldn't believe what I was seeing. Is this even possible? What were the chances of so many trucks, hitched in tandem, being on the expressway together at the exact same time that I would be sitting on the passenger's side of the same SUV that was involved in the incident that caused the very panic attacks and anxiety that I was trying to overcome? I felt like David the shepherd boy being pushed into an entire army of Goliaths.

As we approached the trucks, I began to quietly sing the worship song that my "instadaughter" had sent weeks earlier (thank you, Staci W.). Then, I remembered my verse:

> *Don't worry about anything; instead, pray about everything. Tell God what you need and thank him for all he has done. Then you will experience God's peace, which exceeds anything we can understand. His peace will guard your hearts and minds as you live in Christ Jesus.* (Philippians 4:7)

When I stopped singing, I could hear my verse. I wasn't saying the verse, but the verse was speaking to me. I could actually hear my voice saying that verse inside of me. It was as if I was saying it inside myself. Next, an overwhelming sense of peace came over me. Suddenly, I felt as if I was in a soundproof, impenetrable capsule. I've had peace before, but nothing like this. The only way to describe it is "incomprehensible."

We were surrounded by trucks that were doubles connected in tandem and triples connected in tandem, and yet I felt this unexplainable peace. At one point, I looked over at my husband to see if he felt it, too. We seemed to be gliding by the trucks—gliding by in an insulated, indestructible bubble. We were riding in an SUV, but it seemed as if we were riding inside a tank.

When we finally drove through and passed the cluster of trucks, I smiled and said, "Thank you, God. I lift up my hands."

But, guess what? It wasn't over. Throughout that entire six-hour trip, we drove past, around, by, and through more tandem truck traffic than I have ever seen in my life! I was being tested for the entire six hours, and you know what? Still, there was peace.

When we finally reached our destination, I was rejoicing and praising God. I won! I won! I won! That was the victory that God had waiting for me. Then, the thought came to me, "You still have a six-hour ride home, remember?" I lifted my hands and declared my verse again. And you know what? It happened again.

The six-hour return trip was exactly the same: It was filled with peace. All peace. Nothing but peace! I was able to read, sleep, relax, or chat all the way home—for all six hours—as we whizzed past trucks and trucks whizzed past us.

This was the victory, the win I prepared for. This was me fighting for my rights, fighting for my opportunity to be living proof. I wanted to be able to tell you that it's God's will for you to win in every area of your life. If you want to know what a good fight of faith looks like, here it is. This is my opportunity to let you know that no matter what unwanted fact is challenging your life, you now have the ability to lifespeak your way to victory. You have the authority to take the truth of the Word of God, meditate on it to the point of producing faith, then speak that truth to your unwanted fact and make that fact bow! You're not supposed to win only sometimes. I don't believe in "you win some, you lose some." *No!* That's not your story. You're supposed to win . . . *every time—Period.*

What kept me going? How did I finally get the victory? How did I finally *win*? This is why I wrote this book and included the messy details of this particular story of mine.

It's why I provided all the other examples of exactly how to *do* the Word and not just *hear* the Word. This is faith with works, and it's alive, powerful, and active. Some faith challenges may take more determination on your part than others, but don't give up. Stick with the Word. I had to do it. And the following verses, provided in both the New International Version (NIV) of the Bible and what I call the Life-Speak 101 Amplified Version (LSK101AV), explain why.

Galatians 6:9

NIV: *Let us not become weary in doing good, for at the proper time we will reap a harvest if we do not give up.*

LSK101AV: *I did not get weary in doing good (in this case, meditating), for at the proper time or as other translations call it "due season" (when my faith was sufficiently strong enough in that verse), I knew I would reap a harvest (of overcoming the anxiety of being a car passenger on the expressway) if I didn't cave in or quit (meditating before I received my victory, my win).*

Philippians 1:6

NIV: *Being confident of this, that he who began a good work in you will carry it on to completion until the day of Christ Jesus.*

LSK101AV: *I was fully persuaded that He who began a good work (the work of freedom from anxiety) in me would bring it to completion in Jesus Christ.*

John 8:32

NIV: *Then you will know the truth, and the truth will set you free.*

LSK101AV: *I knew the truth, and the truth that I knew (and applied, folks, you have to apply it) would make me anxiety-free!*

I John 4:4

NIV: *You, dear children, are from God and have overcome them, because the one who is in you is greater than the one who is in the world.*

LSK101AV: *Greater is He (God, and His Word) who is in me than he (or what, like anxiety) who is in the world.*

LifeSpeak 101: Aftermath

We began this journey together by asking some difficult questions based on an unwanted fact: Why is it that Christians, in general, are not winning enough in life? Why are we experiencing the same troubles as non-Christians and seemingly not getting on the other side of them any faster? If we're supposed to be "more than conquerors," where's our victory?

We've determined that it is possible to know all the Bible verses about being conquerors and still live a life that reflects little to none of that victory God's Word promises us.

But now, thanks to this journey called *LifeSpeak 101: Speak Life and Win!*, we know that the distance between reading a verse about victory and getting that victory transferred from the Bible into your life is eliminated through meditation. This journey has taught us that meditation is how faith is manufactured. Once you have faith, you can speak God's Word with power. Getting to that power has been the focus of this book: Lifespeaking is speaking God's Word with power.

The journey of life is filled with ups and downs for everyone, but for those who know the power of the Word of God and are able to lifespeak, they can come out of those downs to a higher place than they ever imagined. We'll all experience challenging times in life. No matter how much we enjoy the sunshine, we know that, at some point, rain is going to come.

The good news is, when the rain begins to fall, we don't have to stand there and get wet. We have an umbrella, and it's called "lifespeaking." So, when we take God's Word and speak it with faith, we not only erect a shield from the rain, but we also make the rainy facts of life bow to the truth of God's Word.

So, what's next for you? Will you walk away from this book without applying its content to your life? Will you be the person who knows the truth but doesn't use it? Now that you know *how* to lifespeak, will you do it? Will you take the steps you've learned and go for the win?

Remember how, when Jesus taught the multitudes and his disciples, he spoke in parables? Then, after the lesson was completed, the disciples would, somehow, have an opportunity to practice what Jesus had taught them. Well, friend, you have that opportunity right here, right now.

The Bible says, "We are to be doers of the Word and not just hearers only" (James 1:22). It also says, "Faith, without works, is dead" (James 2:20).

So, now, it's your turn. What facts are you facing that need to be conformed to the truth of God's Word? In what area(s) of your life do you need to lifespeak, right now, and get a win? Do you need:

- A better job or promotion?
- A more loving marriage?
- An increase in your finances?
- An improvement in your health?
- A restored relationship?

Haven't you waited long enough? Stop waiting! Start today.

Remember, the key is to stick with it. Stand strong. Hold on to the truth and make the facts bow. You can do this! I believe in you!

I'd absolutely love to hear from you and hear about all the ways you're winning and making progress. Share your story by sending your victory reports to @wilmahollislifespeak on Instagram.

Thank you for reading and spending your valuable time with me on this journey. God has an awesome plan for you, and today is just the beginning.My name is Wilma Hollis, and it is my distinct honor to be the first to say . . . *congratulations!* You just completed:

LifeSpeak 101: Speak Life and Win!

Your LifeSpeak Journey Begins

Where do we go from here? Every syllable in this book has been written with the intention of helping you win in every area of your life by speaking God's Word with power. In the following pages, I've provided a template for you to follow the steps you've learned. It provides an easy way for you to map out the journey to your life of victory. Where do you want to begin? What area of your life do you want to change first? Now that you know the steps, do the work. Make the effort. Don't wait. Start your lifespeak journey today and win!

Unwanted Fact: What's the unwanted fact in your life that you are ready to change? Describe it here: (e.g., Unforgiveness)

_____

1. **Watch your words.** Remember: The journey to changing your unwanted fact begins with your commitment to watch your words. Don't say anything negative about your situation. Keep your words positive or keep your mouth shut until you can only speak God's Word about it.

2. **Find your truth.** What does the Word of God say about your unwanted fact? What is the location of the truth you've found to make that fact bow? Write the location of the truth here: (e.g., Colossians 3:13)

_____

3. **Make it yours.** How will you meditate?

Suggestions:

- Write it out. Write it once here and at least five additional times on the page provided.

- Create a screen saver of the verse for your laptop, cell phone, or other devices. Write it on an index card to keep in your pocket or purse. Write it on a Post-it note and attach it to the refrigerator. Make up a song from the verse to sing to yourself.

Remember: The idea is to meditate on that truth (keep it before your eyes, in your ears, and coming out of your mouth to get it in your heart) so that it becomes more real to you than your unwanted facts. This is how you elevate it from being the truth to your truth. (e.g., Bearing with one another and, if one has a complaint against another, forgiving each other; as the Lord has forgiven you, so you also must forgive.)

Write your truth here:

_____

_____

_____

_____

_____

_____

_____

_____

_____

"Make the Truth Yours"
Meditation Sheet

In the space provided, write the verse as many times as possible to fill this page and make it yours. Physically writing it out can keep you from getting distracted and will help you focus on the truth of the scripture or verse and the power it contains to change the unwanted fact(s) in your life.

_____

_____

_____

_____

_____

_____

_____

_____

_____

_____

_____

_____

_____

_____

_____

_____

4. **LifeSpeak** . . .What's your lifespeak declaration? Now that you've made the truth your truth, you've got the faith it takes to lifespeak! (e.g., I forgive others because the Lord has forgiven me.) Remember, this is what you are going to say and declare no matter how you feel, how things look, or what people say. This is the only thing you're going to say about your unwanted fact until the facts bow to the truth of God's Word. You're going to keep lifespeaking until you win!

Write your lifespeak declaration here:

_____

_____

_____

_____

_____

and win! Describe your victory here. Tell me what happened. Exactly how did God keep His Word? What's the best part of your victory? What would you say to someone who thinks this won't work for them? How does it feel now that you've taken that unwanted fact and made it bow to the truth of God's Word?

Tell us how you won:

_____

_____

_____

_____

_____

_____

Now, Let's Stay Connected!

Let me hear from you!

There is victory in your future, and I'd be honored to continue to encourage you along the way. We can stay connected when you subscribe and follow me on these platforms:

- **Instagram:** @WilmaHollisLifeSpeak
- **Twitter:** @WilmaHollis
- **YouTube:** LifeSpeakTV
- **Website:** WilmaHollis.com

You are, officially, a LifeSpeaker! Now, go! Get your victory! You *are ready to win!*

CPSIA information can be obtained
at www.ICGtesting.com
Printed in the USA
LVHW011923140821
695338LV00010B/683